Vocabulary Connections

© Harcourt Achieve Inc.

All Rights Reserved. No part of the material protected by this copyright may be reproduced or utilized in any form or by any means, in whole or in part, without permission in writing from the copyright owner. Requests for permission should be mailed to: Paralegal Department, Harcourt Achieve, P.O. Box 26015, Austin, Texas 78755.

Rigby and Steck-Vaughn are trademarks of Harcourt Achieve Inc. registered in the United States of America and/or other jurisdictions.

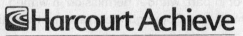

Harcourt Achieve
Rigby • Steck-Vaughn

www.HarcourtAchieve.com
1.800.531.5015

ILLUSTRATIONS

Cover: Ed Lindlof
Content Area Logos: Skip Sorvino

Ben Anglin 102–105, 107; Chris Celusniak 66–68, 70; Holly Cooper 42–44, 46, 60–63, 65, 95–98, 100; Adolph Gonzalez 12–15, 17, 49–50, 52; David Griffin 23–26, 28, 36–39, 41, 78–81, 83, 120–122, 124; John Hartwell 54–57, 59; Mike Krone 114–116, 118; Donna Loughran 18–20, 22; Panne Parker 90–92, 94; Lori Sears 71–74, 76, 84–87; Kay Wilson 6–9, 11, 31, 33, 35, 108–111, 113.

PHOTOGRAPHY

p. 29 © Richard Hutchings/PhotoEdit; pp. 30, 32 © The Bettmann Archive; pp. 47–48 © NASA; p. 53 © Larry Lefever/Grant Heilman Photography; p. 77 © Arthur C. Smith III/Grant Heilman Photography; p. 101 © NASA; p. 119 © Will & Deni McIntyre/Photo Researchers.

Additional photography by Brand X/Getty Royalty Free.

ACKNOWLEDGMENTS

A Guest Is a Guest, by John Himmelman, copyright © 1991 by John Himmelman. Adapted and reprinted by permission of Dutton Children's Books, a division of Penguin Books USA Inc.

Lazy Lion, by Mwenye Hadithi, copyright © 1990 by Bruce Hobson and Adrienne Kennaway. Adapted and reprinted by permission of Little, Brown and Company.

No Place for a Pig, by Phyllis Root and Carol A. Marron, copyright © 1984 by Phyllis Root and Carol A. Marron. Adapted and reprinted by permission of Steck-Vaughn Company.

TABLE OF CONTENTS

CONTENT AREA SYMBOLS

 Literature   Social Studies   Science   Mathematics   Health   Fine Arts

CELEBRATIONS

Celebrations are on special, happy days. They happen at important times, such as your birthday or the new year. They often help us remember people and things from long ago.

In Lessons 1–4, you will read about four different celebrations. Think of a celebration you know about. What did you do? Think about words that tell about this celebration. Write your words on the lines below.

What I Did

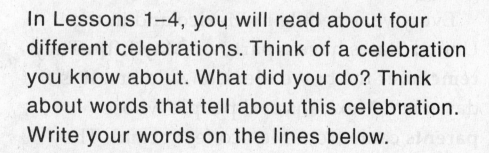

★ Read the story below. Think about the meanings of the words in **dark print**. ★

A Day to Celebrate

Dancing women in bright, pretty dresses spin around and around. The happy sound of Mexican music rings out. The smell of food fills the air. It's Cinco de Mayo!

Cinco de Mayo means the fifth of May in Spanish. Why do people have a party on this day? On May 5, 1862, there was an important **battle** in Mexico. The leader, or **ruler**, of France sent **soldiers** to take over Mexico. On this day, the French soldiers came upon some Mexican soldiers. The French had many men. The Mexicans had few men. The Mexicans had only a few old guns to use to **protect** themselves. But they were **brave**. They didn't give up. In the end, they won the battle!

Every year people in Mexico and in the United States have a party on May fifth. They **remember** the brave Mexican soldiers. It is a day when Mexicans and people whose **parents** came from Mexico feel **proud**. They watch Mexican dances, listen to Mexican music, and eat Mexican food. Cinco de Mayo is a day of fun for everyone!

★ Go back to the story. Underline the words or sentences that give you a clue to the meaning of each word in **dark print**. ★

USING CONTEXT

Meanings for the vocabulary words are given below. Go back to the story, and read each sentence that has a vocabulary word. If you still cannot tell the meaning, look for clues in the sentences that come before and after the one with the vocabulary word. Write each word in front of its meaning.

remember	soldiers	battle	brave
parents	proud	ruler	protect

1. _____: mothers and fathers

2. _____: a big fight with many people

3. _____: not afraid

4. _____: think of something from the past; keep in mind

5. _____: people who fight in a group

6. _____: someone who leads a group of people

7. _____: to keep from being hurt

8. _____: feeling good about who you are or something you have done

DICTIONARY SKILLS

Look at the words in each group. Write them on the lines in ABC order. If you need help, use the alphabet below.

1. battle _____

   music _____

   dance _____

   proud _____

2. ruler _____

   car _____

   brave _____

   think _____

3. soldiers _____

   animals _____

   day _____

   parents _____

4. protect _____

   remember _____

   apple _____

   dark _____

A	B	C	D	E	F	G	H	I	J	K	L	M
N	O	P	Q	R	S	T	U	V	W	X	Y	Z

CROSSWORD PUZZLE

Use the clues and the words in the box to finish the crossword puzzle.

| remember | soldiers | battle | brave |
| parents | proud | ruler | protect |

Across

1. to keep from being hurt
4. not afraid
6. think of something from the past
8. people who fight in a group

Down

2. someone who leads a group
3. mothers and fathers
5. feeling good about who you are
7. a big fight with many people

GET WISE TO TESTS

Directions: Look for the word or words that have the same or almost the same meaning as the underlined word. Darken the circle beside your choice.

Tip

Always read all the answer choices. Many choices may make sense. But only one answer choice has the same or almost the same meaning as the underlined word.

1. important <u>battle</u>
   - ○ dance
   - ○ hill
   - ○ fight
   - ○ party

2. <u>ruler</u> of a country
   - ○ name
   - ○ flower
   - ○ leader
   - ○ car

3. brave <u>soldiers</u>
   - ○ fighters
   - ○ doctors
   - ○ teachers
   - ○ sisters

4. <u>protect</u> someone
   - ○ keep safe
   - ○ keep happy
   - ○ keep sad
   - ○ keep quiet

5. <u>brave</u> person
   - ○ not fast
   - ○ not happy
   - ○ not afraid
   - ○ not tall

6. <u>remember</u> the pictures
   - ○ forget
   - ○ hear
   - ○ see
   - ○ think of

7. one of a child's <u>parents</u>
   - ○ mother
   - ○ brother
   - ○ aunt
   - ○ grandfather

8. feeling <u>proud</u>
   - ○ sorry about
   - ○ good about
   - ○ mad about
   - ○ sad about

Writing

Pretend you just got home from a Cinco de Mayo party. Write a story about the party. Tell why it was held and what you did. Use some vocabulary words in your writing.

_____

_____

_____

_____

_____

_____

_____

_____

_____

_____

Turn to "My Word List" on page 131. Write some words from the story or other words that you would like to know more about. Use a dictionary to find the meanings.

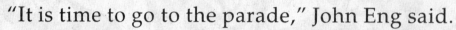

★ Read the story below. Think about the meanings of the words in **dark print**. ★

Dragons in the Street

This story is about two friends who watch the Dragon Parade that Chinese Americans enjoy on New Year's Day.

"It is time to go to the parade," John Eng said.

"Why are we going outside when it is so cold?" asked Mia, John's best friend.

"Because it is Chinese New Year!" John answered. "This year, the Chinese New Year begins on February 10. At least it isn't raining!"

"I don't want to see the dragon parade," Mia said.

"Why not?" John asked. "It will be fun!"

"Dragons scare me!" Mia said.

"No, no," said John. "Dragons are strong and good! They bring us good luck!"

John handed Mia a bright red apple. "Red is the color of good luck. On New Year's Day, we wear good clothes, think good thoughts, and say only kind words. That way, we will have good luck all year!"

Mia looked around. She saw red **decorations** everywhere. "Does everyone have red for good luck?" she asked.

John nodded. He was carrying gifts wrapped in red for his friends.

"See here," he said, "I have little red **envelopes** sealed with a little money inside. These are for my cousins so that they will have good luck in the new year."

"But I don't want to watch the parade!" Mia said.

"Why not?" John asked. "Wasn't it fun? Remember last year when the lion dancers jumped and **pounced**!"

"Yes," Mia agreed. "But now the sharp noise of all the **firecrackers** hurts my ears."

"That's because they are celebrating!" John shouted over the noise, "Come on!"

Men holding long poles weaved and ran through the street. They held a long dragon like a green and gold snake on the poles above their heads. The men **pranced** from side to side. The dragon swept up and down. The dragon was red, green, and gold.

"It's beautiful!" Mia cried.

"Yes," John answered. "Now that the dragon has passed, we will have a **banquet**. Everyone will eat together."

"I feel so silly!" Mia said, "Why was I afraid of the dragon?" The dragon gives good luck to all of us! Now, let's go eat!"

★ Go back to the story. Underline any words or sentences that give you a clue to the meaning of each word in **dark print**. ★

CONTEXT CLUES

Read each sentence. Look for clues to help you finish each sentence with a word from the box. Write the word on the line.

pranced	firecrackers	banquet	evil
pounced	decorations	envelopes	spirits

1. We hung colorful _____ before the party.

2. The children opened the paper _____ to see what was inside.

3. The horse _____ during the whole parade.

4. Do you think _____ spirits can give you bad luck?

5. Everyone ate wonderful food at the Thanksgiving _____.

6. The _____ made a loud noise.

7. The lion _____ on the mouse.

8. Evil _____ were afraid of the lion dancers and the firecrackers.

CLASSIFYING

Study each group of words. Think about how they are alike. Then finish each group with a word from the box. Add another word that you know to each group.

Decorations pounced banquet firecrackers

1. **Times to Eat**
   picnic

   _____

   cookout

   _____

2. **Fireworks**

   _____

   sparklers

   _____

3. **Ways Lion Dancers Moved**
   spun

   _____

   jumped

   _____

4. _____
   balloons
   ribbons
   colored lights

   _____

15

GET WISE TO TESTS

Directions: Read each sentence. Choose the word that best finishes the sentence. Mark the answer space for that word.

Tip

Before you choose an answer, try reading the sentence with each answer choice. This will help you choose an answer that makes sense.

1. The cat _____ on the toy.
   ○ ran   ○ pounced
   ○ played   ○ splashed

2. The letters came in white _____.
   ○ animals   ○ envelopes
   ○ plates   ○ cars

3. They hung _____ for the birthday party.
   ○ clothes   ○ decorations
   ○ plants   ○ pictures

4. Erin was an _____ witch in the school play.
   ○ empty   ○ early
   ○ every   ○ evil

5. Some people believe in _____.
   ○ spirits   ○ homes
   ○ cats   ○ buses

6. We lit _____ on the Fourth of July.
   ○ beaches   ○ firecrackers
   ○ trees   ○ movies

7. The pony _____ at the head of the parade.
   ○ crawled   ○ laughed
   ○ pranced   ○ swam

8. Everyone went to a big _____ to eat good food.
   ○ game   ○ flower
   ○ money   ○ banquet

Writing

For John, New Year's Day is a special day.
What special day is your favorite? What do
you do on that day? Why do you like it? Do
you go somewhere? Do you eat special foods?
Do you see many people?

Use the lines below to write about your
special day. Use some vocabulary words in
your writing.

On my special day, I like to _____

_____

_____

_____

_____

_____

_____

_____

Turn to "My Word List" on
page 131. Write some words
from the story or other words
that you would like to know
more about. Use a dictionary
to find the meanings.

17

★ Read the story below. Think about the meanings of the words in **dark print**. ★

Making Rain

All living things need rain. People who live in dry country need rain most of all. The Hopi people live in the **desert**. Rain is very important to the Hopi. If the rain does not come, their corn will not grow.

The Hopi people get together to ask the spirits for rain. They have a special kind of parade. First comes the leader, then a girl, two boys, and some men. They walk to a **spring** where water comes out of the ground. The leader plays the **flute**, and the other people sing songs asking for rain. Then the leader **dives** into the spring. He swims under the water. There he plants a stick with birds' feathers tied to it in the mud. Then he stands in the water and plays the flute.

The parade returns home. One of the men draws a picture on the **trail** where they walk. He uses corn to draw three cloud **symbols**. Then the girl and boys throw yellow **sunflowers** on the drawing.

After the flute dance, the Hopi **search** the sky. They look for clouds that will bring rain.

★ Go back to the story. Underline the words or sentences that give you a clue to the meaning of each word in **dark print**. ★

USING CONTEXT

Meanings for the vocabulary words are given below. Go back to the story, and read each sentence that has a vocabulary word. If you still cannot tell the meaning, look for clues in the sentences that come before and after the one with the vocabulary word. Write each word in front of its meaning.

sunflowers	spring	desert	flute
symbols	search	dives	trail

1. _____ : land with little water

2. _____ : to look for something

3. _____ : place where water comes from the ground

4. _____ : jumps with the head first

5. _____ : long, round piece of wood or metal that makes music

6. _____ : path through a wild area

7. _____ : large, yellow flowers

8. _____ : pictures and other things that stand for something else

WORD GROUPS

Read each pair of words. Think about how they are alike. Write the word from the box that belongs in each word group.

sunflowers	spring	desert	flute
symbols	search	dives	trail

1. plants, roses, _____

2. road, path, _____

3. river, brook, _____

4. look, watch, _____

5. forest, field, _____

6. swims, floats, _____

7. drum, horn, _____

8. signs, clues, _____

Directions: Darken the circle beside the word that has the same or almost the same meaning as the underlined word.

Tip

If you are not sure which word completes the sentence, do the best you can. Try to choose the answer that makes the most sense.

1. A <u>spring</u> is a place where water comes from the—
   ○ air   ○ ground
   ○ candy   ○ oven

2. To <u>search</u> means to—
   ○ swim   ○ run
   ○ look   ○ cook

3. A <u>flute</u> makes—
   ○ music   ○ honey
   ○ money   ○ snow

4. A <u>trail</u> is a—
   ○ hand   ○ ring
   ○ path   ○ tree

5. A <u>desert</u> is—
   ○ dry   ○ wet
   ○ blue   ○ green

6. <u>Symbols</u> are—
   ○ cats   ○ people
   ○ snakes   ○ signs

7. Someone who <u>dives</u>—
   ○ runs   ○ walks
   ○ climbs   ○ jumps

8. <u>Sunflowers</u> are—
   ○ animals   ○ plants
   ○ people   ○ rocks

Writing

The Hopi people get together to ask for rain. Think about the kind of weather you like. On the lines below, tell about your favorite kind of weather. Tell why you like it. Use some vocabulary words in your writing.

Turn to "My Word List" on page 131. Write some words from the story or other words that you would like to know more about. Use a dictionary to find the meanings.

_____

_____

_____

_____

_____

_____

_____

_____

_____

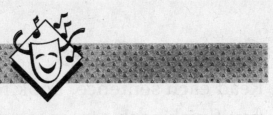

★ Read the story below. Think about the meanings of the words in **dark print**. ★

The Magic of Masks

In almost every African **village**, or small town, there is a **woodcarver**. He makes wooden **masks** that look like faces. The masks can be scary, funny, or beautiful.

The masks are made to be worn. They are kept in a **hut**, or small house. On special days, people wear the masks. They also wear **costumes** that cover their bodies. Then they dance to the sound of drums.

In Africa, there are dances for many things. There is a dance when someone dies. There is a dance to make the **crops** grow. Some dances tell stories about how the world was made.

Most villages have a dance when girls or boys grow up. They use masks in these dances, too. The dances tell the boys and girls to act like **adults**. Then the whole village feels proud of its fine young men and women.

Dances with masks are an important part of life in Africa. Each village uses dances to teach people what is right and wrong. Children learn the **values** of their people from the masks made by the woodcarver.

★ Go back to the story. Underline the words or sentences that give you a clue to the meaning of each word in **dark print**. ★

CONTEXT CLUES

Read each sentence. Look for clues to help you finish each sentence with a word from the box. Write the word on the line.

woodcarver	masks	adults	crops
costumes	values	village	hut

1. Every family has its own small house,

   or _____ .

2. A _____ can make beautiful things out of wood.

3. The woodcarver made some scary

   _____ with wide mouths.

4. Everyone who lives in the

   _____ knows everyone else.

5. Everyone in the village grows

   _____ for food.

6. People wear special _____ for the dance.

7. The _____ hope their children will learn from the dance.

8. Helping your family and your village are

   important African _____ .

SYNONYMS

Synonyms are words that have the same or almost the same meaning. Draw a line under the word in the second sentence that matches the word or words in dark print in the first sentence.

1. There are only ten families in my small **town**.

   I live in a village.

2. My father is **the person who makes wooden things** for the village.

   He is a woodcarver.

3. I stand in front of my **small house** to watch the dance.

   I come out of my hut to see it.

4. The children hope that they can dance when they are **grown-ups**.

   The people who are dancing are adults.

5. The adults wear **special clothes** for the dance.

   These costumes are worn for celebrations.

WORD PUZZLE

Write a word from the box next to each clue. Then read the word made from the boxed letters. The letters in the boxes will spell the word for the last clue.

woodcarver	masks	adults	crops
costumes	values	village	hut

1. I am a small town.
   ☐ __ __ __ __ __ __

2. We look like faces, but we are made of wood or something else.
   __ ☐ __ __ __

3. We are people who are grown up.
   __ __ __ ☐ __ __

4. I am a small house. __ ☐ __

5. I make things out of wood.
   __ __ __ __ __ __ __ __ ☐ __

6. These are plants grown for food.
   __ __ __ ☐ __

7. We are special clothes used for the dances.
   __ __ __ __ __ __ __

8. These are what you believe to be right and wrong. __ __ __ __ __ __

GET WISE TO TESTS

Directions: Darken the oval beside the word
that best finishes the sentence.

On some tests, the answer spaces are <u>not</u> circles.
Be sure to fill in the answer spaces completely.

1. A small town is a . . .
   ○ city   ○ village   ○ country   ○ state

2. A person who makes things out of wood is a . . .
   ○ teacher   ○ driver   ○ mother   ○ woodcarver

3. Faces made of wood are . . .
   ○ hats   ○ smiles   ○ shirts   ○ masks

4. A small house is a . . .
   ○ car   ○ boat   ○ hut   ○ castle

5. Plants grown for food are . . .
   ○ crops   ○ hats   ○ stars   ○ pictures

6. Special clothes worn for celebrations are . . .
   ○ whistles   ○ horns   ○ costumes   ○ pans

7. People who are grown up are . . .
   ○ children   ○ babies   ○ brothers   ○ adults

8. The things you believe are right and wrong are your . . .
   ○ songs   ○ values   ○ stories   ○ jokes

Writing

The picture on this page shows an African mask. Pretend that you are making a mask. How would it look? Draw a picture of your mask in the box.

On the lines below, write about the mask you drew. When would it be worn? Who would wear it? What feelings would it show? Use some vocabulary words in your writing.

_____

_____

_____

_____

_____

Turn to "My Word List" on page 131. Write some words from the story or other words that you would like to know more about. Use a dictionary to find the meanings.

★ To review the words in Lessons 1–4, turn to page 125. ★

HEROES

What makes someone a hero? A hero can be a person who does something no one has ever done before. Most often, a hero is someone who helps many people.

In Lessons 5–8, you will read about four heroes. Do you know about any heroes? Do you have a hero? Think of words that tell about heroes. Write your words on the lines below.

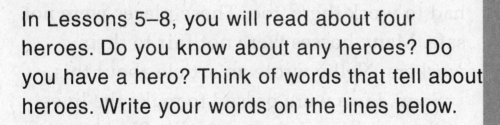

Heroes Are:

_____

_____

_____

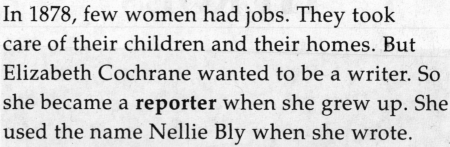

★ Read the story below. Think about the meanings of the words in **dark print**. ★

Nellie Bly

In 1878, few women had jobs. They took care of their children and their homes. But Elizabeth Cochrane wanted to be a writer. So she became a **reporter** when she grew up. She used the name Nellie Bly when she wrote.

Nellie Bly cared about poor people. She went into part of a city where the poorest people lived. She saw many people **crowded** together in old, broken-down buildings. The buildings weren't **safe** to live in. Still, the people who owned them would not **repair**, or fix, them. Nellie wrote an **article** to tell about the buildings. She put her story in the **newspaper** so everyone could read it.

Then Nellie went to see where many of the poor people worked. She found that children had to work there, too. These places were not safe. Many bosses were not **fair** to their workers. Nellie wrote an article about this.

Soon, **laws** were passed to make the lives of the poor people better. Nellie Bly was happy. She helped many people. She led the way for many women to become reporters!

★ Go back to the story. Underline the words or sentences that give you a clue to the meaning of each word in **dark print**. ★

Using Context

Meanings for the vocabulary words are given below. Go back to the story, and read each sentence that has a vocabulary word. If you still cannot tell the meaning, look for clues in the sentences that come before and after the one with the vocabulary word. Write each word in front of its meaning.

| crowded | reporter | repair | laws |
| newspaper | article | safe | fair |

1. _____ : sheets of paper that tell about what just happened

2. _____ : too close to each other

3. _____ : to fix

4. _____ : rules made for all people

5. _____ : person who writes for a newspaper

6. _____ : free from danger

7. _____ : right

8. _____ : a story for a newspaper

CLOZE PARAGRAPH

Use the words in the box to finish the paragraph. Read the paragraph again to be sure it makes sense.

| crowded | reporter | repair | laws |
| newspaper | article | safe | fair |

A (1) _____ is a person who writes stories. These stories are put in a

(2) _____ so people can read them. The stories are (3) _____ on every page. A reporter can tell people if a

building is not (4) _____.
Then the people who own it will have to

(5) _____ it.

A reporter can find out if something is not

right, or (6) _____. Then the

reporter can write an (7) _____ about it. This can help make sure that

(8) _____ are passed to keep it from happening anymore.

WORD RIDDLES

Read each riddle. Use words from the box to answer each riddle.

crowded	reporter	repair	laws
newspaper	article	safe	fair

1. I can fix things.
   What can I do? _____

2. I have stories that tell about what just happened.
   What am I? _____

3. We are too close together.
   What are we? _____

4. I am free from danger.
   What am I? _____

5. I am someone who writes for a newspaper.
   Who am I? _____

6. I am a story in a newspaper.
   What am I? _____

7. I do what is right.
   What am I? _____

8. We are rules for all people.
   What are we? _____

GET WISE TO TESTS

Directions: Read each sentence. Choose the word that best finishes the sentence. Mark the answer space for that word.

Tip Read carefully. Use the other words in the sentences to help you choose each missing word.

1. The _____ won a prize for her story.
   ○ runner   ○ reporter
   ○ nurse   ○ doctor

2. Did you see my picture in the _____?
   ○ flower   ○ letter
   ○ cloud   ○ newspaper

3. The people were _____ together in the small room.
   ○ crowded   ○ written
   ○ jumped   ○ sent

4. It isn't _____ to play with fire.
   ○ happy   ○ wrong
   ○ quiet   ○ safe

5. Megan's dad will _____ her broken bicycle.
   ○ tear   ○ fight
   ○ repair   ○ ride

6. I saw an _____ in the newspaper about schools.
   ○ orange   ○ egg
   ○ article   ○ ant

7. It is not _____ to lie to others.
   ○ fair   ○ mean
   ○ warm   ○ fun

8. _____ help us live together happily.
   ○ Glasses   ○ Laws
   ○ Bats   ○ Cars

Writing

A newspaper reporter is always looking for a good story to write about. A good reporter watches everything that happens around him or her. Then the reporter writes stories about these things.

Pretend you are a newspaper reporter. Tell about something that has just happened. Be sure to tell how, when, why, and where it happened. Then tell what you think about it. Use some vocabulary words in your writing.

The Times

_____
(date)

_____

_____

_____

_____

_____

_____

_____

Turn to "My Word List" on page 131. Write some words from the story or other words that you would like to know more about. Use a dictionary to find the meanings.

35

★ Read the story below. Think about the meanings of the words in **dark print**. ★

What's in a Name?

This story tells about why Martin Luther King, Jr., is important to all of us.

"Our school is named for Martin Luther King, Jr.," said Mr. Diaz. "Does anyone know why so many schools and roads are named for Martin Luther King, Jr.?"

That question made Marty think. His name was Martin, too.

"There is even a holiday for Martin Luther King, Jr. It is on the third Monday of January every year," the teacher said.

"It is because he had a great name!" Marty said. He felt **excited** because he and Martin Luther King, Jr. had the same first name.

Mr. Diaz laughed. "That may be," he said. "But our school was named for Martin Luther King, Jr. for the same reason that other schools and streets are named for George Washington and Abraham Lincoln."

"They were presidents," Angela said.

"Yes," said Tommy, "but there were other presidents."

"Tommy is right," Mr. Diaz said. "But George Washington and Abraham Lincoln were great men. They made things **change** in our country. So did Martin Luther King, Jr."

Mr. Diaz **described** how Martin Luther King, Jr., grew up in Atlanta, Georgia, in the 1930s. At the time, African American children could not go to the same schools as white children. Even though they might be friends, African American and white children sometimes got in trouble for playing together. African American children could not eat in the same places as white children. They could not even drink from the same water fountains. They had to live **apart**.

All his life, Martin Luther King, Jr., had a **dream**. His dream was that someday people would all be equal. When African Americans and whites were not treated the same, he became **upset**. He wanted to do something about it.

But he was always **calm** as he worked for change. He worked hard to make the laws change. Thanks to his hard work, children today all can go to the same schools.

"Think about Martin Luther King, Jr., when you come to school in the morning," Mr. Diaz said. "He was brave. He worked to make the world a better place for everyone. He wanted to bring people together. How can you be like Martin Luther King, Jr.?"

★ Go back to the story. Underline any words or sentences that give you a clue to the meaning of each word in **dark print**. ★

USING CONTEXT

Meanings for the vocabulary words are given below. Go back to the story, and read each sentence that has a vocabulary word. If you still cannot tell the meaning, look for clues in the sentences that come before and after the one with the vocabulary word. Write each word in front of its meaning.

join	upset	dream	described
calm	apart	change	excited

1. _____ : unhappy

2. _____ : told about or written about

3. _____ : not together

4. _____ : very happy

5. _____ : a wish

6. _____ : come together with

7. _____ : to become different

8. _____ : quiet and still

ANTONYMS

Antonyms are words with opposite meanings. Circle the word or words in the sentence that are an antonym of the word in dark print.

upset

1. Mike was very happy that his mother and father were taking him to the fair.

apart

2. He always has a good time when they are together.

calm

3. When they got to the fair, Mike's favorite ride wasn't there! He was very upset.

excited

4. Mike was sad because he couldn't go on the ride.

change

5. Mike asked his mother and father why the fair didn't stay the same every year.

GET WISE TO TESTS

Directions: Look for the word or words that have the same or almost the same meaning as the underlined word. Darken the circle beside your choice.

Tip

Always read all the answer choices. Many choices may make sense. But only one answer choice has the same or almost the same meaning as the underlined word.

1. calm voice
   - quiet
   - happy
   - sad
   - angry

2. excited winner
   - sad
   - angry
   - new
   - happy

3. miles apart
   - not happy
   - not together
   - not old
   - not hot

4. upset child
   - young
   - glad
   - unhappy
   - smart

5. described the house
   - smiled about
   - told about
   - cleaned about
   - thought about

6. join your friends
   - come down
   - come together
   - come through
   - come away

7. tried to change
   - become sad
   - become bad
   - become different
   - become good

8. your dream
   - wish
   - glass
   - puddle
   - house

Writing

Martin didn't think it was fair that black and white children couldn't go to school together. When he grew up, he helped to change that. Is there something you would like to change?

On the lines below, write about something you would like to change someday. What would you change? How would you change it? Use some vocabulary words in your writing.

_____

_____

_____

_____

_____

_____

_____

_____

Turn to "My Word List" on page 131. Write some words from the story or other words that you would like to know more about. Use a dictionary to find the meanings.

_____

_____

_____

★ Read the story below. Think about the meanings of the words in **dark print**. ★

Player with a Heart

Roberto Clemente loved baseball. As a child in Puerto Rico, he played baseball often. When Roberto was 19, he went to the United States to play baseball. His first years there were hard. People could not **understand** Roberto because he spoke Spanish. Many baseball players acted differently toward him because he was black. But people saw that he was a great player. People liked him because he worked hard and told the **truth**.

Roberto loved children. He often visited sick children in **hospitals**. He knew what it was like to be in **pain**. His back and his **elbow**, where the arm bends, often hurt.

In 1972, there was an **earthquake** that shook the earth. It left many people without homes. Roberto collected food, money, and **medicine** for those who were sick or hurt. On December 31, Roberto got on an airplane to help the people. Soon after taking off, the airplane **crashed**. Roberto Clemente was killed. The world had lost both a great baseball player and a great man.

★ Go back to the story. Underline the words or sentences that give you a clue to the meaning of each word in **dark print**. ★

CONTEXT CLUES

Read each sentence. Look for clues to help you finish each sentence with a word from the box. Write the word on the line.

| earthquake | medicine | crashed | truth |
| understand | hospitals | elbow | pain |

1. At first, many people could not

_____ Roberto because he

spoke Spanish.

2. Roberto's mother and father told him to

tell the _____.

3. Sick children in _____ were

glad to see Roberto.

4. The children forgot their_____

when Roberto was visiting.

5. Sometimes, Roberto's _____

hurt so much he couldn't play baseball.

6. Roberto wanted to help the people who lost

their homes in the _____.

7. Roberto knew the people who were hurt

would need _____.

8. Roberto died when his airplane

_____.

SYNONYMS

Synonyms are words that have the same or almost the same meaning. Find the word in the box that means the same or almost the same as the underlined word or words. Write the word on the line.

understand	hospitals	elbow
medicine	crashed	pain

1. Doctors and nurses <u>know</u> how to help people get well.

   _____

2. They care for sick people in <u>special buildings</u>.

   _____

3. Doctors give people <u>shots</u> to help them get well.

   _____

4. Jennifer <u>fell down</u> when she was riding her bicycle.

   _____

5. She hurt her <u>arm where it bends</u>.

   _____

6. The doctors and nurses at the hospital soon helped her <u>feeling of being hurt</u> go away.

   _____

Directions: Darken the oval beside the word that best finishes the sentence.

Tip Read carefully. Use the other words in the sentences to help you choose each missing word.

1. To know something well is to . . . it.
   ○ think   ○ forget   ○ teach   ○ understand

2. If you don't lie, you tell the . . .
   ○ light   ○ truth   ○ mark   ○ sound

3. Places where sick people are cared for are . . .
   ○ houses   ○ rooms   ○ hospitals   ○ schools

4. A feeling of hurt is . . .
   ○ pain   ○ help   ○ love   ○ smile

5. The place where the arm bends is the . . .
   ○ elbow   ○ back   ○ face   ○ head

6. When the earth moves and shakes, it is called an . . .
   ○ apple   ○ orange   ○ earthquake   ○ egg

7. Something a doctor gives you to help you get well is . . .
   ○ candy   ○ medicine   ○ food   ○ cake

8. If a kite fell to the ground, it . . .
   ○ crashed   ○ rolled   ○ flew   ○ stopped

Writing

Roberto Clemente was a great baseball player. He also helped many people. This made him a great man. Many people looked up to him.

Think of someone you know who helps people. What does this person do? How does he or she help people? On the poster below, draw a picture of this special person. Then write a short paragraph on the lines below telling about this great person.

Turn to "My Word List" on page 131. Write some words from the story or other words that you would like to know more about. Use a dictionary to find the meanings.

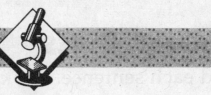

★ Read the story below. Think about the meanings of the words in **dark print**. ★

Riding into Space

When Sally Ride was a child, she wanted to be an **astronaut**. She dreamed of flying into space. But Sally didn't think her dream would come true. At that time, all the American astronauts were men.

When Sally grew up, she **studied** to learn about the stars. She also studied **planets**, such as Earth. One day Sally read in the newspaper that new astronauts were needed. Sally wrote a letter, and she was picked.

Sally needed many hours of **training** to learn to be an astronaut. She learned what to do during the **flight** into space. At last Sally flew on the **shuttle** *Challenger*, a spaceship with wings. Sally helped put **satellites** into space to go around the earth. These machines sent pictures to Earth. She also did many **experiments** to find out about things in space.

Sally was the first American woman to travel in space. Most people think she is special because of this. But Sally doesn't think she is any more important than the other astronauts.

★ Go back to the story. Underline the words or sentences that give you a clue to the meaning of each word in **dark print**. ★

CONTEXT CLUES

Read each sentence. Look for clues to help you finish each sentence with a word from the box. Write the word on the line.

| experiments | satellites | studied | shuttle |
| astronaut | training | planets | flight |

1. An _____ is someone who flies into space.

2. Astronauts need much _____.

3. They must do _____ to learn how things happen.

4. They must know how _____ can send pictures back to Earth.

5. Sally Ride _____ hard to become an astronaut.

6. She knows about many _____, including Earth.

7. Few people ever get to fly in a space

_____.

8. Every astronaut hopes to be picked for a

shuttle _____.

WORD GROUPS

Read each pair of words. Think about how they are alike. Write the word from the box that best finishes each word group.

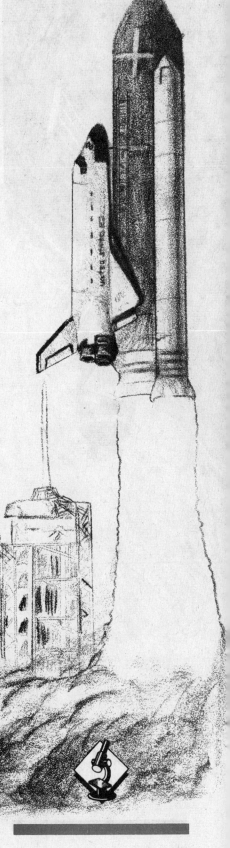

| experiments | satellites | studied | shuttle |
| astronaut | training | planets | flight |

1. teacher, doctor, _____

2. fly, flying, _____

3. moon, stars, _____

4. airplane, spaceship, _____

5. thought, read, _____

6. teaching, learning, _____

7. tests, tries, _____

8. machines, pictures, _____

49

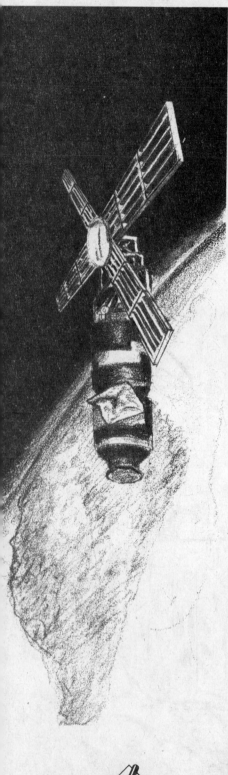

WORD CODES

A **code** is a kind of secret writing. Each letter stands for a different letter.

A vocabulary word is written in code above each clue. Use the box at the bottom of the page to find out each coded word. Write your answer on the spaces above the letters.

| experiments | planets |
| astronaut | shuttle |

1. _ _ _ _ _ _ _
 k o z m v g h
bodies in space that move around the sun

2. _ _ _ _ _ _ _ _ _
 z h g i l m z f g
a person who flies into space

3. _ _ _ _ _ _ _
 h s f g g o v
a spaceship with wings that can be used many times

4. _ _ _ _ _ _ _ _ _ _ _
 v c k v i r n v m g h
tests to find out something

a=z	b=y	c=x	d=w	e=v	f=u	g=t
h=s	i=r	j=q	k=p	l=o	m=n	n=m
o=l	p=k	q=j	r=i	s=h	t=g	u=f
v=e	w=d	x=c	y=b	z=a		

GET WISE TO TESTS

Directions: Darken the circle beside the word or words that have the same or almost the same meaning as the underlined word or words.

Tip Before you choose an answer, try reading the sentence with each answer choice. This will help you choose an answer that makes sense.

1. A person who flies into space is an—
   ○ airplane   ○ ice skater
   ○ author   ○ astronaut

2. If you tried to learn you—
   ○ played   ○ studied
   ○ jumped   ○ ran

3. Round bodies in space are—
   ○ planets   ○ cars
   ○ balls   ○ trains

4. The act of flying is called—
   ○ class   ○ school
   ○ flight   ○ thought

5. A spaceship with wings is a—
   ○ person   ○ shuttle
   ○ road   ○ wagon

6. Machines in space are—
   ○ moons   ○ satellites
   ○ stars   ○ suns

7. Teaching that you give to a person is called—
   ○ saying   ○ doing
   ○ thinking   ○ training

8. Tests to find out something are—
   ○ experiments ○ cars
   ○ animals   ○ plants

Writing

Sally Ride wanted to be an astronaut when she grew up. She had to work very hard to become an astronaut.

On the lines below, tell what you want to do when you grow up. Tell why you want to do this. Tell if you will need special training. Use some vocabulary words in your writing.

_____

_____

_____

_____

_____

_____

_____

_____

_____

_____

_____

Turn to "My Word List" on page 131. Write some words from the story or other words that you would like to know more about. Use a dictionary to find the meanings.

★ To review the words in Lessons 5–8, turn to page 126. ★

ON THE FARM

A farm is a home for many different kinds of animals. There are many sights to see and many sounds to hear.

In Lessons 9–12, you will read about farms. What animals do you think live on a farm? What sounds do you think you would hear on a farm? Think about words that tell about those sounds. Write your words on the lines below.

Farm Sounds

_____

_____

_____

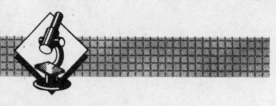

★ Read the story below. Think about the meanings of the words in **dark print**. ★

Animals on a Farm

The red rooster crows loudly. The **farmer** smiles as he eats his eggs and ham and drinks his milk. This food came from the animals he cares for when he does his **chores** each day.

There is a large **herd** of cattle eating grass in the **pasture**. Many of the cattle are dark red. They will go to **market** and be sold for meat. The other cattle are black and white. The farmer gets milk from these cattle.

The pigs are sleeping in their pen. They are quite fat. They will be ready for market soon. The farmer gets meat from the pigs.

The farmer must **raise** sheep where crops won't grow. You can often see a **flock** of many sheep **grazing** on a hill. The farmer gets meat and wool from the sheep. Their soft wool is used to make rugs and clothes.

The hens are eating corn on the ground. The rooster watches over the hens. The hens lay eggs. The eggs are white, brown, or spotted. Many of the eggs are sold at the market.

The farmer works hard to care for his animals. But they give him much in return!

★ Go back to the story. Underline the words or sentences that give you a clue to the meaning of each word in **dark print**. ★

USING CONTEXT

Meanings for the vocabulary words are given below. Go back to the story, and read each sentence that has a vocabulary word. If you still cannot tell the meaning, look for clues in the sentences that come before and after the one with the vocabulary word. Write each word in front of its meaning.

| farmer | chores | herd | pasture |
| market | raise | flock | grazing |

1. _____ : a group of sheep or birds

2. _____ : work that must be done each day

3. _____ : grassy land that animals use for food

4. _____ : a person who works on a farm

5. _____ : a group of large animals

6. _____ : help something grow

7. _____ : eating grass

8. _____ : a place where farmers sell animals and other things

MULTIPLE MEANINGS

The words in the boxes have more than one meaning. Look for clues in each sentence to tell which meaning is used. Write the letter of the meaning next to the correct sentence.

herd **a.** a group of large animals **b.** to join together	1. _____ The farmer will herd the animals into the barn.
	2. _____ There is a herd of cattle.
raise **a.** lift up **b.** help to grow	3. _____ I raise the flag every morning.
	4. _____ My aunt will raise pigs and chickens.
flock **a.** a group of sheep or birds **b.** to go in a group	5. _____ I saw a flock of ducks yesterday.
	6. _____ People will flock to the party.
grazing **a.** lightly touching **b.** eating grass	7. _____ There are cattle grazing in that field.
	8. _____ Her sleeve was grazing the top of the desk.

Handwritten annotations: READ/STudy, verb, noun-group, verb, verb, group, verb, group, touching, ex. Fish eats fish food.

56

WORD MAP

Words can be put on a kind of map to show that they are alike. Write each word from the box in the group where it belongs to tell about farm animals. Then add a word you know to each group.

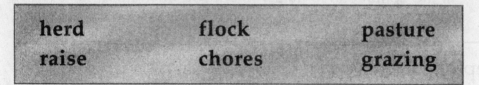

herd	flock	pasture
raise	chores	grazing

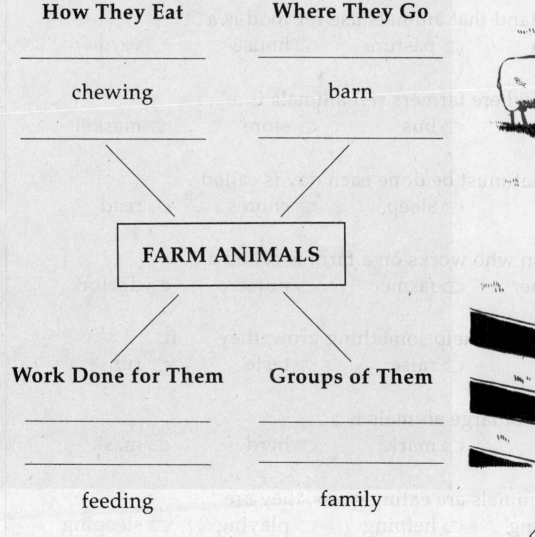

How They Eat

_____

chewing

_____

Where They Go

_____

barn

_____

FARM ANIMALS

Work Done for Them

_____

feeding

_____

Groups of Them

_____

family

_____

GET WISE TO TESTS

Directions: Darken the oval beside the word that best finishes the sentence.

 Read each sentence carefully. Use the other words in the sentences to help you choose each missing word.

1. A group of sheep or birds is a . . .
   ○ flock   ○ class   ○ family   ○ school

2. Grassy land that animals use for food is a . . .
   ○ room   ○ pasture   ○ house   ○ yard

3. A place where farmers sell animals is a . . .
   ○ field   ○ bus   ○ store   ○ market

4. Work that must be done each day is called . . .
   ○ play   ○ sleep   ○ chores   ○ read

5. A person who works on a farm is called a . . .
   ○ teacher   ○ farmer   ○ nurse   ○ doctor

6. When people help something grow, they . . . it.
   ○ see   ○ raise   ○ taste   ○ run

7. A group of large animals is a . . .
   ○ map   ○ mark   ○ herd   ○ mask

8. When animals are eating grass, they are . . .
   ○ grazing   ○ helping   ○ playing   ○ sleeping

Writing

You have raised your farm animal since it was a baby. You have worked very hard caring for it. Now the big moment has come. You and your animal have just won the prize at the farm animal show!

On the lines below, write about your farm animal. What kind of animal is it? What color is it? What are some things you like best about it? Tell how you took care of your farm animal each day. Use some vocabulary words in your writing.

_____

_____

_____

_____

_____

_____

_____

_____

_____

_____

_____

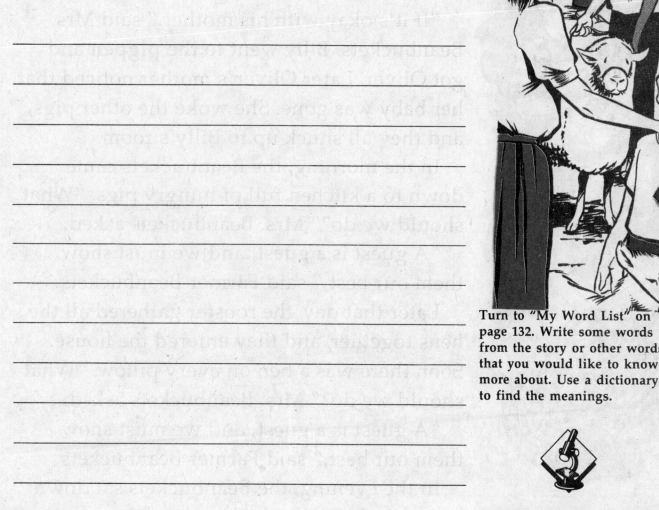

Turn to "My Word List" on page 132. Write some words from the story or other words that you would like to know more about. Use a dictionary to find the meanings.

59

★ Read the story below. Think about the meanings of the words in **dark print**. ★

A Guest Is a Guest

In this story, farm animals are treated like part of the farmer's family.

Farmer Beanbuckets, his wife, and their son, Billy, lived on a farm. The Beanbuckets always treated their animals like part of the family. Billy was **fond** of a clever little baby pig named Oliver. One **evening**, Billy asked if he could have a friend spend the night.

"If it's okay with his mother," said Mrs. Beanbuckets. Billy went to the **pigpen** and got Oliver. Later Oliver's mother noticed that her baby was gone. She woke the other pigs, and they all snuck up to Billy's room.

In the morning, the Beanbuckets came down to a kitchen full of hungry pigs. "What should we do?" Mrs. Beanbuckets asked.

"A guest is a guest, and we must show them our best," said Farmer Beanbuckets.

Later that day, the rooster gathered all the hens together, and they entered the house. Soon there was a hen on every pillow. "What should we do?" Mrs. Beanbuckets asked.

"A guest is a guest, and we must show them our best," said Farmer Beanbuckets.

In the evening, the Beanbuckets sat down to watch their favorite **western**. The sound of the TV western brought the horses and cows **stampeding** into the room.

"More guests?" asked Billy.

"Afraid so," said Farmer Beanbuckets.

Now the house was filled with animals. They took over the TV. They ate all the good stuff out of the refrigerator.

Finally, Farmer Beanbuckets cried, "A guest is a guest, and we must show them our best, but when enough is enough, you have to get tough!" So the animals threw the Beanbuckets out.

Then Billy had an idea. He called Oliver outside to the pigpen. When Oliver's mother saw them, she led the pigs out of the house, where they could keep a better eye on Oliver.

This gave Farmer Beanbuckets an idea. He jumped onto a **perch** in the chicken **coop**. "Cockadoodleydoo," he crowed. The rooster didn't like someone else doing his job, and he led the hens out to the coop.

Mrs. Beanbuckets rolled the TV into the **stable**. The horses and cows followed her.

The Beanbuckets ran back into the house and locked the door behind them. "A guest is a guest, and now it's time for some rest," said Farmer Beanbuckets.

From <u>A Guest Is a Guest</u>, by John Himmelman

★ Go back to the story. Underline any words or sentences that give you a clue to the meaning of each word in **dark print**. ★

CONTEXT CLUES

Read each sentence. Look for clues to help you finish each sentence with a word from the box. Write the word on the line.

western	**fond**	**perch**	**evening**
pigpen	**coop**	**stable**	**stampeding**

1. The Beanbuckets were _____ of their animals.

2. One of Billy's morning chores was feeding the horses in the _____.

3. Billy lived in the house, but Oliver lived outside in the _____.

4. The rooster crowed from his _____ every morning.

5. The Beanbuckets' hens laid many eggs in the chicken _____.

6. The Beanbuckets watched TV after their _____ meal.

7. The show they watched was a _____.

8. They saw horses _____ on the show.

DICTIONARY SKILLS

Look at the words in each group. Write them on the lines in ABC order. If you need help, use the alphabet below.

1. coop _____

   pigpen _____

   apple _____

   zoo _____

2. evening _____

   cow _____

   wall _____

   stable _____

3. fond _____

   orange _____

   crab _____

   lion _____

4. perch _____

   horse _____

   western _____

   town _____

A B C D E F G H I J K L M
N O P Q R S T U V W X Y Z

GET WISE TO TESTS

Directions: Darken the circle beside the word that has the same or almost the same meaning as the underlined word or words.

Tip

Use each answer choice in place of the underlined word or words. Remember that the underlined word or words and your answer must have the same meaning.

1. Evening is—
   ○ night   ○ book
   ○ car   ○ day

2. A stable is a kind of—
   ○ house   ○ school
   ○ horse   ○ chair

3. A coop is a house for—
   ○ pigs   ○ horses
   ○ cattle   ○ chickens

4. A perch is a—
   ○ branch   ○ hill
   ○ dog   ○ car

5. A place for pigs is a—
   ○ pigpen   ○ story
   ○ food   ○ doctor

6. A western is a kind of—
   ○ apple   ○ door
   ○ movie   ○ foot

7. To be fond is to—
   ○ see   ○ like
   ○ use   ○ read

8. Stampeding cattle are—
   ○ running   ○ sleeping
   ○ walking   ○ jumping

Writing

The Beanbuckets had a problem. They wanted their house back. They worked together to get the animals to leave their house.

Look at the picture. It shows a different way the Beanbuckets could have fixed their problem.

Write a paragraph telling how <u>you</u> would have fixed the problem. Use some vocabulary words in your writing.

_____

_____

_____

_____

_____

_____

_____

_____

_____

_____

_____

_____

_____

Turn to "My Word List" on page 132. Write some words from the story or other words that you would like to know more about. Use a dictionary to find the meanings.

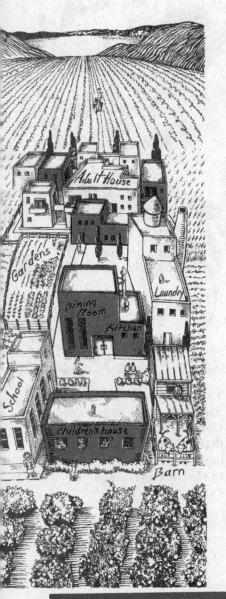

★ Read the story below. Think about the meanings of the words in **dark print**. ★

Teaming Up

You see people working together on a farm. But instead of "Hello!" you hear "Shalom!" Where are you? You are on a **kibbutz**, or special farm, in Israel.

A kibbutz is a home for many farmers. Its **members** share everything. They raise crops and animals together. They even make their **clothing** and **furniture** together in the kibbutz **factories**.

Life on a kibbutz is very busy. Everyone has a job. The boys work in the fields or in the factories. The girls care for the children. Some adults cook or wash dishes. Others help wash clothes in the **laundry**. Even the young children have jobs. Some take care of the vegetable **gardens**. Others **tend** the animals. All the children go to school on the kibbutz.

The families live apart. There are special houses for the children. The parents live in other houses. But they visit each other every day. They also eat together in a big dining room. The families live apart, but they always share the food they've grown together.

★ Go back to the story. Underline the words or sentences that give you a clue to the meaning of each word in **dark print**. ★

CONTEXT CLUES

Read each sentence. Look for clues to help you finish each sentence with a word from the box. Write the word on the line.

clothing	laundry	kibbutz	tend
furniture	members	factories	gardens

1. A _____ is a special farm in Israel.

2. We must go get the clean clothes from the _____ .

3. My parents bought _____ for my bedroom.

4. Farmers _____ many crops and animals.

5. We packed warm _____ for the trip.

6. My art club has ten _____ .

7. There are many _____ in our town where clothes are made.

8. There are beautiful _____ around the library.

CLOZE PARAGRAPH

Use the words in the box to finish the paragraph. Reread the paragraph to be sure it makes sense.

clothing	laundry	kibbutz	tend
furniture	members	factories	gardens

My name is Gadi, and I am from Israel. I live with my family in Tel Aviv. Tel Aviv is a large city by the sea. My family is made up of

five (1) _____. My mom and

dad grew up on a (2) _____.

They worked in the (3) _____ when they were children. Their parents

washed clothes in the (4) _____. But they wanted to live in the city.

Today they are both teachers. My sister, Rina, works in a shop that sells baby

(5) _____. Moshe, my brother,

works at two (6) _____. He

makes wooden (7) _____ at both places.

As for me, I go to school each day. I also

(8) _____ Rami, my dog. I make sure he always has food and water. I think I am very lucky. I have the best family in the whole world.

Directions: Read each sentence. Choose the word that best finishes the sentence. Mark the answer space for that word.

Tip Read carefully. Use the other words in the sentences to help you choose each missing word.

1. Farmers like growing things. Perhaps that is why they live on a _____.
   ○ hill   ○ kibbutz
   ○ road   ○ horse

2. Tamar is in the youth club on the kibbutz. The club has many _____.
   ○ arms   ○ circles
   ○ dogs   ○ members

3. The gardens are very large. The children must _____ many vegetables.
   ○ run   ○ tend
   ○ walk   ○ throw

4. There are many clothes to keep clean on a kibbutz. The people in the _____ wash the clothes.
   ○ laundry   ○ smile
   ○ kitchen   ○ sky

5. The kibbutz needs many clothes for its people. Most are made in its _____.
   ○ tents   ○ schools
   ○ factories   ○ houses

6. The laundry workers wash clothes all day. They take care of everyone's _____.
   ○ cats   ○ letters
   ○ sisters   ○ clothing

7. You will find many beds and chairs in the children's house. But there is no other _____ there.
   ○ circus   ○ sheep
   ○ furniture   ○ food

8. The adults cook the meals on the kibbutz. They use food from the _____.
   ○ games   ○ stars
   ○ ducks   ○ gardens

Writing

Pretend that you are living on a kibbutz. You must do your job and work hard like everyone else. Where would you work? In a factory? In the kitchen? In the gardens? Maybe you would work in the barn because you like animals. Maybe you would work in the kitchen because you like to cook.

Write down your two favorite jobs. Tell about the kinds of things you would do in each job. Use some vocabulary words in your writing.

Turn to "My Word List" on page 132. Write some words from the story or other words that you would like to know more about. Use a dictionary to find the meanings.

Job 1 _____

_____

_____

_____

_____

_____

Job 2 _____

_____

_____

_____

_____

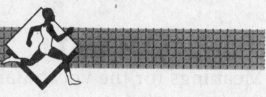

★ Read the story below. Think about the meanings of the words in **dark print**. ★

In the Fields

A bird flies high above the corn field. The **tractor** begins to hum. The farmer drives the tractor toward the long rows of corn. As he begins to pick the corn, long-eared rabbits run for safety. The farmer is happy. He is ready to pick all the **grain** he grew this year. Another **harvest** has begun!

At harvest time in the fall, the colors in the fields change. Then the farmer picks the corn. Next he picks oats and wheat. During the harvest, the farmer works very hard and gets much **exercise**. He will need plenty of **rest** at night. He must have a good **diet** and plenty of the best foods. He will need enough **energy** to load all the grain onto a truck. The farmer will use the truck to take the grain to the market.

The grain will be used in many foods. The wheat, corn, and oats will be used to make bread and cereal. These foods are part of a **healthy** diet.

The farmer feels proud. He knows many people will enjoy the food from his harvest.

★ Go back to the story. Underline any words or sentences that give you a clue to the meaning of each word in **dark print**. ★

USING CONTEXT

Meanings for the vocabulary words are given below. Go back to the story, and read each sentence that has a vocabulary word. If you still cannot tell the meaning, look for clues in the sentences that come before and after the one with the vocabulary word. Write each word in front of its meaning.

| diet | tractor | harvest | exercise |
| rest | grain | energy | healthy |

1. _____: wheat, oats, and corn

2. _____: a machine used on a farm

3. _____: the foods a person eats every day

4. _____: the picking of crops

5. _____: not sick

6. _____: sleep

7. _____: the power to work

8. _____: moving of the body in work or play

SYNONYMS

Synonyms are words that have the same or almost the same meaning. Read each sentence. Circle the word or words that are a synonym for the word in dark print.

tractor   1. Tom drives his farm machine almost every day.

harvest   2. He uses the tractor for the picking of crops.

diet   3. He also makes sure he eats good food every day.

exercise   4. All this work keeps him in shape.

rest   5. Tom makes sure he gets all the sleep he needs.

energy   6. He has the power to work because he has a good diet.

grain   7. He eats cereal made of wheat, oats, and corn.

healthy   8. Tom is not sick very often because he does all these things.

CROSSWORD PUZZLE

Use the clues and the words in the box to finish the crossword puzzle.

diet	grain	harvest	exercise
rest	tractor	healthy	energy

Across

1. the foods a person eats every day
3. the picking of crops
5. wheat, oats, and corn
7. moving of the body in work or play

Down

2. a machine used on a farm
4. the power to work
6. not sick
8. sleep

GET WISE TO TESTS

Directions: Look for the word that has the same or almost the same meaning as the underlined word or words. Darken the circle beside your choice.

1. kind of grain
   ○ meat   ○ cheese
   ○ butter   ○ wheat

2. the picking of crops
   ○ movie   ○ harvest
   ○ night   ○ winter

3. the power to work
   ○ sad   ○ hurt
   ○ energy   ○ fun

4. get some rest
   ○ jump   ○ sleep
   ○ skip   ○ climb

5. the foods you eat
   ○ diet   ○ potatoes
   ○ peas   ○ apples

6. moving of the body in work or play
   ○ sheep   ○ sports
   ○ weather   ○ exercise

7. not sick
   ○ healthy   ○ sorry
   ○ silly   ○ tired

8. machine on a farm
   ○ train   ○ plane
   ○ bus   ○ tractor

Writing

Farming is hard work. Farmers do chores every day. Just like the farmers, you do many things every day.

Do you also have chores? Do you do homework? Do you care for a pet? On the lines below, tell about the things you do every day. Tell why you do these things. Tell which things you like best. Use some vocabulary words in your writing.

_____

_____

_____

_____

_____

_____

_____

_____

_____

_____

_____

_____

_____

Turn to "My Word List" on page 132. Write some words from the story or other words that you would like to know more about. Use a dictionary to find the meanings.

★ To review the words in Lessons 9–12, turn to page 127. ★

HOME SWEET HOME

People and animals live in different kinds of homes. Some animals live in trees or in caves. Some animals build their own homes.

In Lessons 13–16, you will read about different kinds of homes. Think about your home. What do you like about it? What are your favorite things in your home? Think of words that tell about your home. Write your words under the heading below.

My Home

_____

_____

_____

77

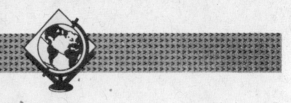

★ Read the story below. Think about the meanings of the words in **dark print**. ★

Where You Live

Who are the people in the **neighborhood** where you live? Do you know the people who live next door or across the street?

If you live in the city, you probably have many **neighbors** who live around you. Many people in the city live in **apartments**. If you live in an apartment, you may know your neighbors across the hall. There may be neighbors above you or below you. But the people who live across the street from your apartment may be **strangers**. *Don't know them*

If you live in the country, you may not be able to see your neighbor's house. But if you look out your **bedroom** window, you may be able to see their cattle.

There are many places to go and many things to see in a neighborhood. There may be a **playground** where you like to play. There may be a **grocery** store where you can buy food or a good **restaurant** where you can eat.

All neighborhoods are different. But in some ways, they are all the same. Your neighborhood is part of your life.

★ Go back to the story. Underline the words or sentences that give you a clue to the meaning of each word in **dark print**. ★

CONTEXT CLUES

Read each sentence. Look for clues to help you finish each sentence with a word from the box. Write the word on the line.

neighborhood	bedroom	neighbors
apartments	strangers	playground
restaurant	grocery	

1. My family and I ate dinner at a very nice

   _____.

2. People you do not know are

   _____.

3. I know many people in the

   _____ where I live.

4. My friend and I went shopping at the

   _____ store.

5. My grandmother gave me a new blanket that matches everything in my

   _____.

6. I like to go down the slide at the

   _____.

7. My _____ who live across the street are my best friends.

8. I have two close friends who live in

   _____ down the street.

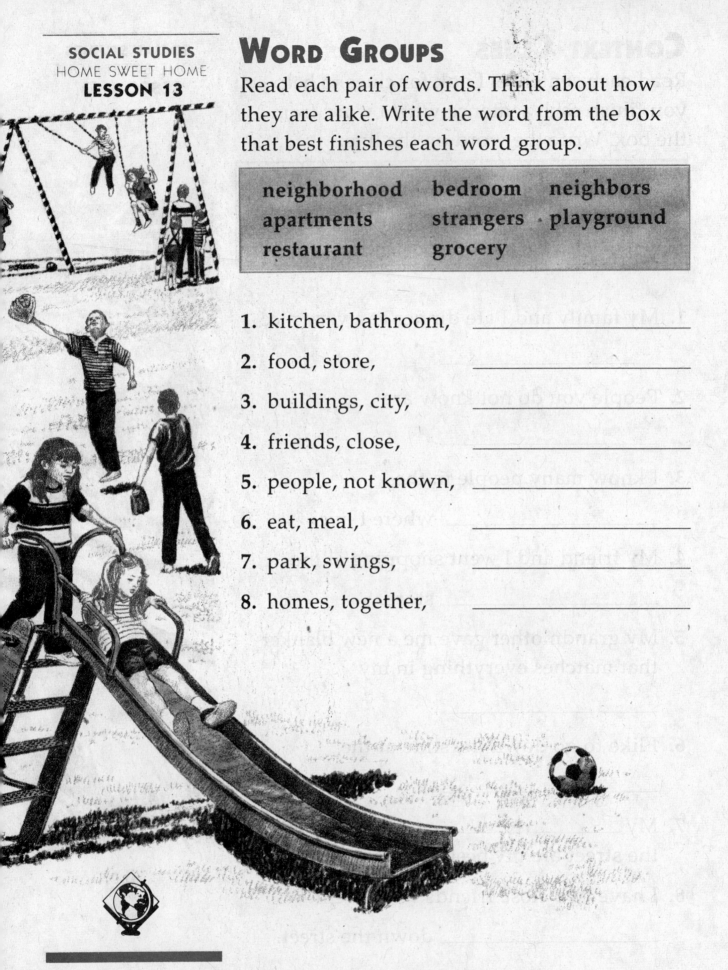

WORD GROUPS

Read each pair of words. Think about how they are alike. Write the word from the box that best finishes each word group.

neighborhood	bedroom	neighbors
apartments	strangers	playground
restaurant	grocery	

1. kitchen, bathroom, _____

2. food, store, _____

3. buildings, city, _____

4. friends, close, _____

5. people, not known, _____

6. eat, meal, _____

7. park, swings, _____

8. homes, together, _____

WORD GAME

Write a word from the box under each clue. Then read the word made by the boxed letters. It names a place with many neighborhoods.

bedroom	neighbors
strangers	playground
grocery	restaurant

1. a store that sells food

   ___ ___ ___ ___ [ ] ___ ___ ___

2. people who live in the next house or nearby

   ___ ___ [ ] ___ ___ ___ ___ ___ ___

3. a place to buy and eat a meal

   ___ ___ ___ [ ] ___ ___ ___ ___ ___ ___

4. a place for outdoor play

   ___ ___ ___ [ ] ___ ___ ___ ___ ___ ___

5. people not known, seen, or heard of before

   ___ ___ ___ ___ ___ ___ ___ ___ ___

6. a room to sleep in

   ___ ___ ___ ___ ___ ___ ___

81

GET WISE TO TESTS

Directions: Darken the oval beside the word that best finishes the sentence.

Tip Read each sentence carefully. Use the other words in the sentences to help you choose each missing word.

1. A room where you sleep is a . . .
   ○ classroom   ○ bedroom   ○ bathroom   ○ kitchen

2. People who live in the next house or nearby are your . . .
   ○ neighbors   ○ children   ○ parents   ○ sisters

3. A store that sells food is a . . .
   ○ pet   ○ toy   ○ grocery   ○ book
     store   store   store   store

4. People you do not know are . . .
   ○ strangers   ○ teachers   ○ parents   ○ friends

5. A place for outdoor play is a . . .
   ○ store   ○ library   ○ playground ○ city

6. Large buildings with groups of rooms to live in are . . .
   ○ houses   ○ schools   ○ apartments ○ barns

7. A place to buy and eat a meal is a . . .
   ○ restaurant ○ farm   ○ house   ○ store

8. A place where people live near one another is a . . .
   ○ school   ○ farm   ○ neighborhood ○ street

Writing

Every neighborhood is different. There are many things to see and do. What is your favorite place in your neighborhood? Draw a picture of this place in the space below.

Write a note to a friend inviting him or her to your favorite place. Tell what you will do and how much fun it will be. Use some vocabulary words in your writing.

Turn to "My Word List" on page 132. Write some words from the story or other words that you would like to know more about. Use a dictionary to find the meanings.

★ Read the story below. Think about the meanings of the words in **dark print**. ★

No Place for a Pig

This story tells what could happen if you had a pet pig.

The day Cynthia the pig **gobbled** the garbage, knocked over the bookshelf, and broke down the bed, Peter's mother said, "This house is no place for a pig!"

So Peter washed Cynthia, packed her favorite pillow, and set out to find her another place to live.

Peter liked Mrs. Mallory's garden. "Just **imagine** yourself here," he said. "You could sniff the daisies and nap in the shade."

But the daisies made Cynthia's nose itch. She could only imagine herself **wheezing** and scratching. She tugged Peter down the street.

"How about the school?" he asked. "I can picture you rolling in the grass and playing tag with the children."

Cynthia peeked in the window. The children were in art class. She could picture herself being painted and pasted. She **dragged** Peter along the street.

Peter thought the **diner** might work. "Can you see yourself here?" he asked. "You could chew the steak bones and **munch** on the potato peels."

But the cook was making ham and beans, and everyone looked hungry. Cynthia could see herself being **roasted** and toasted. She pulled Peter away.

Peter thought the church was too quiet. Cynthia thought the bowling alley was too noisy. And both of them knew the meat market would never do. The only place left was the woods.

"I don't know," said Peter. "Do you think you could be happy here? You could root in the leaves and search for friends in the dark."

Just then something rustled in the woods, something hissed in the woods, and something **howled** in the woods. They both raced all the way home.

"Mom, I'm back," yelled Peter. "I looked everywhere, but I couldn't find another home for Cynthia."

Peter's mother gave them both a big hug. "Come outside," she said. "Cynthia's grown too big for this house. But she still belongs here with us."

"Cynthia knew that all along," said Peter. "And so did I." He helped his mother nail on the last boards. Together they tucked Cynthia and her pillow inside her new house.

From No Place for a Pig, by Phyllis Root and Carol A. Marron

★ Go back to the story. Underline any words or sentences that give you a clue to the meaning of each word in **dark print**. ★

USING CONTEXT

Meanings for the vocabulary words are given below. Go back to the story, and read each sentence that has a vocabulary word. If you still cannot tell the meaning, look for clues in the sentences that come before and after the one with the vocabulary word. Write each word in front of its meaning.

| imagine | diner | dragged | gobbled |
| howled | munch | roasted | wheezing |

1. _____: to chew loudly

2. _____: cooked in an oven

3. _____: ate fast

4. _____: pulled along

5. _____: a place to eat

6. _____: to pretend or to make a picture of something in the mind

7. _____: having a hard time breathing

8. _____: cried loudly and for a long time

SYNONYMS

Synonyms are words that have the same or almost the same meaning. Read each sentence. Draw a line under the word or words that are a synonym for the word in dark print.

roasted 1. The meat was baked in the oven.

dragged 2. The heavy box was pulled across the floor.

gobbled 3. She was so hungry that she ate very fast.

wheezing 4. The firefighters were having a hard time breathing in the smoke.

imagine 5. My friend likes to pretend that she is a teacher.

diner 6. We ate lunch at a small restaurant.

munch 7. When the cow was grazing, we could hear her chew loudly.

howled 8. The dog cried loudly all night long.

GET WISE TO TESTS

Directions: Look for the word that has the same or almost the same meaning as the underlined word or words. Darken the circle beside your choice.

Tip Always read all the answer choices. Many choices may make sense. But only one answer choice has the same or almost the same meaning as the underlined word or words.

1. He <u>ate</u> fast.
   ○ ran
   ○ gobbled
   ○ fell
   ○ slept

2. She <u>pulled</u> me down the street.
   ○ dragged
   ○ pushed
   ○ carried
   ○ lifted

3. We like to <u>pretend</u> we are grown up.
   ○ think
   ○ imagine
   ○ like
   ○ sell

4. We ate at a nice <u>restaurant</u>.
   ○ school
   ○ park
   ○ diner
   ○ car

5. The dog <u>cried</u> loudly.
   ○ sang
   ○ howled
   ○ thought
   ○ played

6. You should not <u>chew</u> loudly.
   ○ munch
   ○ drink
   ○ laugh
   ○ cry

7. It was <u>baked in</u> an oven.
   ○ cold
   ○ wet
   ○ roasted
   ○ gone

8. He is having a <u>hard time</u> breathing.
   ○ wheezing
   ○ drinking
   ○ growing
   ○ eating

Writing

Peter had a pet pig named Cynthia. Do you have a pet? What kind of animal would you like to have for a pet?

What would you say to your mother or father so you could have this pet? On the lines below, tell why your pet would be a good pet. Use some vocabulary words in your writing.

_____

_____

_____

_____

_____

_____

_____

_____

_____

Turn to "My Word List" on page 132. Write some words from the story or other words that you would like to know more about. Use a dictionary to find the meanings.

_____

_____

★ Read the story below. Think about the meanings of the words in **dark print**. ★

A House Built of Sticks

People live in homes built by **carpenters**. The carpenters use tools to build these homes. But animals are different. Many live in trees or in caves. But **beavers** are animals that build very special homes.

A beaver's home is called a **lodge**. It is built in a pond or a lake. This lodge is made from sticks and mud. There is a **cozy** room inside where the beaver lives. This room is above the water and stays warm and dry. The lodge protects the beaver from the cold. The beaver is safe from its **enemies** because the only door to its lodge is under the water. The beaver swims under the water and climbs up into the lodge.

Sometimes the beaver cannot find a pond or a lake. So it builds a **dam** across a stream. The beaver cuts down trees with its teeth. Then it uses the trees, sticks, and mud to make a dam. The dam **blocks** the water to make a pond for the beaver's lodge.

Beavers build **amazing** homes. Maybe someday you will get to see a beaver home.

★ Go back to the story. Underline the words or sentences that give you a clue to the meaning of each word in **dark print**. ★

CONTEXT CLUES

Read each sentence. Look for clues to help you finish each sentence with a word from the box. Write the word on the line.

lodge	beavers	cozy	carpenters
blocks	enemies	dam	amazing

1. Animals that build their own homes are

   _____.

2. A beaver home is called a

   _____.

3. A beaver home is _____ and warm.

4. Beavers are safe from their

   _____ in their homes.

5. A beaver home is an _____ sight.

6. A beaver _____ water in a stream to make a pond.

7. Beavers build a _____ across the stream.

8. People who build houses are called

   _____.

CLOZE PARAGRAPH

Use the words in the box to finish the paragraph. Read the paragraph again to be sure it makes sense.

lodge	beavers	cozy	carpenters
blocks	enemies	dam	amazing

There are (1) _____ who have jobs building homes for people. But (2) _____ are animals that build their own homes. They build (3) _____ homes in a pond or a lake. A beaver home is called a (4) _____. A beaver builds this lodge out of sticks and mud. The room inside the lodge is (5) _____ and dry. The lodge keeps the beaver warm and protects it from its (6) _____.

What happens when a beaver cannot find a pond or a lake? Then it makes a pond. The beaver (7) _____ a stream with sticks, logs, and mud. This is called a (8) _____. Then the beaver can build its lodge.

Directions: Read each sentence. Choose the word that best finishes the sentence. Mark the answer space for that word.

Tip

Read carefully. Use the other words in the sentence to help you choose each missing word.

1. _____ are animals that build their own homes.
   - ○ Beavers
   - ○ Cats
   - ○ Dogs
   - ○ Bears

2. A beaver home is called a _____.
   - ○ house
   - ○ lodge
   - ○ room
   - ○ cave

3. A beaver home is an _____ sight.
   - ○ amazing
   - ○ ugly
   - ○ easy
   - ○ open

4. A _____ is made of sticks, logs, and mud.
   - ○ pond
   - ○ tree
   - ○ dam
   - ○ ground

5. A dam _____ water to make a pond.
   - ○ lets
   - ○ freezes
   - ○ blocks
   - ○ sees

6. People live in homes built by _____.
   - ○ beavers
   - ○ children
   - ○ animals
   - ○ carpenters

7. A beaver home is _____ and warm.
   - ○ cozy
   - ○ hard
   - ○ cold
   - ○ lost

8. The door under the water helps protect beavers from their _____.
   - ○ babies
   - ○ enemies
   - ○ friends
   - ○ brothers

Writing

People and animals live in many different kinds of homes. Pretend that you are building your own home. You can make it from anything you like. Maybe you would use ice, pizza, or books. Draw a picture of your home in the space below.

Write a story telling about your home. Where will you build it? What is it made from? Who will live with you? Use some vocabulary words in your writing.

_____

_____

_____

_____

_____

_____

_____

Turn to "My Word List" on page 132. Write some words from the story or other words that you would like to know more about. Use a dictionary to find the meanings.

★ Read the story below. Think about the meanings of the words in **dark print**. ★

A Home in the Ground

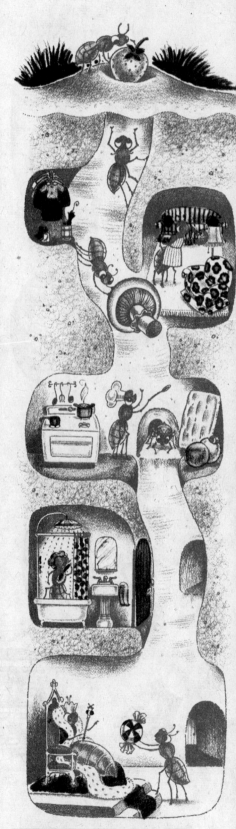

Did you know ants are like people? They work together to get things done. Ants live in a large group called a **colony**. **Hundreds** of ants live in each colony. Each ant has its own job. Together the ants help their colony grow. Most ant colonies are in the ground. A colony has many cozy little rooms.

Most ants in a colony are worker ants. They find food, care for the baby ants, and make the colony bigger. Worker ants are very strong. If a worker ant finds food that is too big to carry, other worker ants help. But a **single** worker ant can carry something 50 times its own **weight**. That would be the same as a person being able to **lift** an elephant!

The worker ants also care for the **queen** ant. Her job is to lay eggs. This is the only thing she does. There may be one or more queens in each colony. They live for 5 to 15 **years**. During that time, each queen lays **thousands** of eggs. These eggs become baby ants. This makes much work for the worker ants. It's no wonder that ants are everywhere!

★ Go back to the story. Underline the words or sentences that give you a clue to the meaning of each word in **dark print**. ★

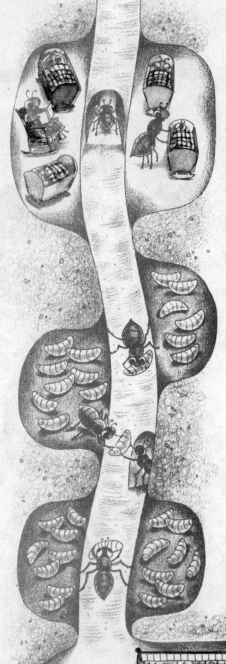

USING CONTEXT

Meanings for the vocabulary words are given below. Go back to the story, and read each sentence that has a vocabulary word. If you still cannot tell the meaning, look for clues in the sentences that come before and after the one with the vocabulary word. Write each word in front of its meaning.

colony	weight	thousands	queen
lift	single	hundreds	years

1. _____ : to pick up

2. _____ : more than 12 months

3. _____ : how heavy something is

4. _____ : an ant that lays eggs

5. _____ : more than 1,000

6. _____ : a group of ants living together

7. _____ : more than 100

8. _____ : only one

CLASSIFYING

Study each group of words. Think about how they are alike. Then finish each group with a word or words from the box. Add another word that you know to each group.

| thousands | colony | queen |
| hundreds | years | |

1. **Numbers**
   tens

   _____

   _____

   _____

2. **Time**
   days

   _____

   _____

3. **Rulers**
   king

   _____

   _____

4. **Places to Live**
   house

   _____

   lodge

   _____

CROSSWORD PUZZLE

Use the clues and the words in the box to finish the crossword puzzle.

colony	weight	thousands	queen
lift	single	hundreds	years

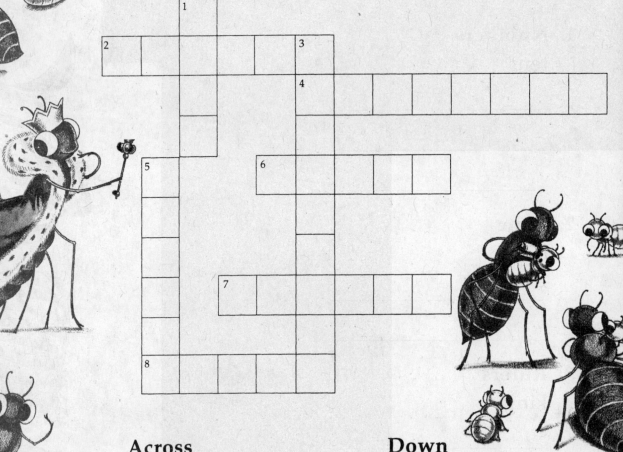

Across

2. how heavy something is
4. more than 100
6. an ant that lays eggs
7. only one
8. more than 12 months

Down

1. to pick up
3. more than 1,000
5. group of ants

Directions: Darken the circle beside the word that has the same or almost the same meaning as the underlined word or words.

Tip

Use each answer choice in place of the underlined word or words. Remember that the underlined word or words and your answer must have the same or almost the same meaning.

1. Only one is—
   ○ single   ○ two
   ○ small   ○ five

2. How heavy something is is its—
   ○ head   ○ weight
   ○ arm   ○ age

3. To pick up is to—
   ○ lift   ○ count
   ○ talk   ○ think

4. Something that lasts more than 12 months lasts—
   ○ days   ○ weeks
   ○ tens   ○ years

5. An ant that lays eggs is a—
   ○ parent   ○ teacher
   ○ child   ○ queen

6. A group of ants is a—
   ○ house   ○ colony
   ○ bird   ○ person

7. More than 100 is—
   ○ hundreds   ○ tens
   ○ fives   ○ twos

8. More than 1,000 is—
   ○ tens   ○ thousands
   ○ threes   ○ fours

Ants are very tiny. Pretend that you are as small as an ant. What do you think it would be like to be so small? What does your home look like? How do you feel? What do you do?

Write a story about yourself on the lines below. Use some vocabulary words in your writing.

_____

_____

_____

_____

_____

_____

_____

_____

_____

_____

_____

_____

_____

_____

Turn to "My Word List" on page 132. Write some words from the story or other words that you would like to know more about. Use a dictionary to find the meanings.

★ To review the words in Lessons 13–16, turn to page 128. ★

AROUND THE WORLD

No place on earth is quite like any other. Every place looks, sounds, and smells a little different. Many kinds of plants, animals, weather, and land make the world an interesting place.

In Lessons 17–20, you will read about different parts of the world. Pretend you are taking a trip around the world. What kinds of things would you see? Write your words on the lines below.

What I Would See

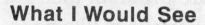

★ Read the story below. Think about the meanings of the words in **dark print**. ★

Land Down Under

Why is Australia called the Land Down Under? Because it is on the bottom half of the earth! North America is on the top half of the earth. When it is winter in North America, it is **summer** in Australia.

Australia is a **continent**. It is a big piece of land with **oceans**, or seas, all around it. Australia is also a country. It is the only country in the world that is also a continent.

Australia is a special place. There are plants and animals there that don't live anywhere else. **Kangaroos** are animals that live in Australia.

Australia is so dry that most of the **rivers** and lakes there only have water in them for part of the year. There are **huge** deserts in Australia. Most of these deserts are sandy. The wind piles the sand into large **dunes**.

Most people in Australia live on the **coast**. More rain falls on this edge of the land close to the oceans. The people are proud of their country. They know that Australia is like no other place in the world.

★ Go back to the story. Underline any words or sentences that give you a clue to the meaning of each word in **dark print**. ★

CONTEXT CLUES

Read each sentence. Look for clues to help you finish each sentence with a word from the box. Write the word on the line.

kangaroos	summer	rivers	coast
continent	oceans	dunes	huge

1. Australia is both a country and a

   _____.

2. If you go there during Australia's

   _____, take clothes for

   warm weather.

3. You could fly over the deserts and see the

   sand _____.

4. You could feed the _____.

5. You could go to the _____
   by the sea to see the water.

6. You could catch many fish in the

   _____ around Australia.

7. You could see the many

   _____ and lakes in
   Australia, but they only have water in
   them part of the year.

8. Australia is too _____ to
   see in one trip!

WORD GROUPS

Read each pair of words. Think about how they are alike. Write the word from the box that best finishes each word group.

kangaroos	summer	rivers	huge
continent	oceans	dunes	coast

1. winter, spring, _____

2. springs, streams, _____

3. hills, sand, _____

4. big, large, _____

5. land, country, _____

6. lakes, seas, _____

7. lions, ducks, _____

8. land, edge, _____

CROSSWORD PUZZLE

Use the clues and the words in the box to finish the crossword puzzle.

| kangaroos | summer | rivers | huge |
| continent | oceans | dunes | coast |

Across

2. animals with strong back legs for jumping

3. large streams of water

7. hills of sand

8. large bodies of water

Down

1. a very large piece of land

4. the warmest part of the year

5. very large

6. the land along the sea

GET WISE TO TESTS

Directions: Darken the circle beside the word that has the same meaning as the underlined word or words.

Tip

Before you choose an answer, try reading the sentence with each answer choice. This will help you choose an answer that makes sense.

1. During the <u>summer</u>, it is—
   ○ warm   ○ cold
   ○ dark   ○ icy

2. A <u>continent</u> is a piece of—
   ○ water   ○ land
   ○ food   ○ grass

3. <u>Oceans</u> are—
   ○ cars   ○ hills
   ○ houses   ○ seas

4. <u>Kangaroos</u> are—
   ○ people   ○ things
   ○ animals   ○ schools

5. Something that is very <u>large</u> is—
   ○ small   ○ little
   ○ cold   ○ huge

6. <u>Sand hills</u> are—
   ○ dunes   ○ ponds
   ○ trees   ○ lakes

7. <u>The land along the sea</u> is the—
   ○ farm   ○ city
   ○ coast   ○ road

8. <u>Large streams of water</u> are called—
   ○ seas   ○ rivers
   ○ ponds   ○ hills

Writing

What is the land like where you live? Is it flat or hilly? Is it dry, or are there rivers and lakes? What plants and animals live there?

On the lines below, tell about the land where you live. Use some vocabulary words in your writing.

_____

_____

_____

_____

_____

_____

_____

_____

_____

_____

_____

Turn to "My Word List" on page 132. Write some words from the story or other words that you would like to know more about. Use a dictionary to find the meanings.

★ Read the story below. Think about the meanings of the words in **dark print**. ★

Lazy Lion

In this African story, Lazy Lion tries to find a house.

When the first clouds appeared above the hot African plains, Lazy Lion roared, "The Big Rain is coming. I will need a roof to keep me dry. And since I am the King of the **Beasts**, I will order a fine house to be built."

So he went to the Weaver Birds. "Build me a house," he ordered. "A big house!" The Weaver Birds built a nest of grasses and palm leaves, and it hung from the branch of a tree. But Lazy Lion was too heavy to reach the door. "I won't live up a tree," said Lion crossly.

So he went to the **Aardvarks**. "Build me a house," he ordered. "A big house!" The Aardvarks dug a huge hole with many rooms and caves. But it was so dark that Lion couldn't see anything. "I won't live underground," said Lion crossly.

So he went to Honey **Badger**. "Build me a house," he ordered. "A big house!" Honey Badger found a **hollow** tree stump and ate all the bees and honey inside it, and cleaned it as clean as clean, and Lion climbed inside. But his head stuck out of the hole in the top, and his tail stuck out of the hole at the bottom.

"I won't live in a tree stump," said Lion crossly.

So he went to **Crocodile**. "Build me a house," he ordered. "A big house!" Crocodile found a cave in the **riverbank** and swept it with his tail, and Lion walked in and went to sleep. But in the night the cave filled with water from the river. "I won't live in the water," said Lion crossly.

By now Lazy Lion was very, very angry, and the sky was full of big black clouds. So Lion called all the animals together. "You must ALL build me a house," he ordered. "A VERY, VERY BIG…" But just then there was a flash of lightning in the sky, and a **rumbling** of thunder, and suddenly the Big Rain poured down everywhere.

The Aardvarks rushed underground. Honey Badger hurried off to his tree stump. Crocodile **waddled** into his cave. The Weaver Birds flapped to their nest. And they all watched Lion sitting in the rain in the middle of the African plain.

"He is so very difficult to please," said Crocodile. And he cried a few tears. Not real ones. Just little crocodile ones.

To this day, Lion has not found a house to live in. So he just wanders the African plain.

From Lazy Lion, by
Mwenye Hadithi

★ Go back to the story. Underline any words or sentences that give you a clue to the meaning of each word in **dark print**. ★

109

USING CONTEXT

Meanings for the vocabulary words are given below. Go back to the story, and read each sentence that has a vocabulary word. If you still cannot tell the meaning, look for clues in the sentences that come before and after the one with the vocabulary word. Write each word in front of its meaning.

aardvarks	crocodile	waddled	badger
riverbank	rumbling	hollow	beasts

1. _____ : any animals with four legs

2. _____ : the ground beside a river

3. _____ : animals that dig large holes to live in

4. _____ : having nothing inside

5. _____ : an animal with many sharp teeth that lives near a river

6. _____ : a deep, heavy sound

7. _____ : an animal that eats bees and honey

8. _____ : walked with short steps

CLOZE PARAGRAPH

Use the words in the box to finish the paragraph. Read the paragraph again to be sure it makes sense.

aardvarks	crocodile	waddled	badger
riverbank	rumbling	hollow	beasts

All the (1) _____ except Lazy Lion had their own houses. The

(2) _____ lived under the

ground. The (3) _____ had a home that filled with water at night. He lived

in the (4) _____. The

(5) _____ lived in the stump of a tree. The tree stump was

(6) _____, or empty inside. When the Big Rain came, all the animals

walked or (7) _____ into their

houses. But Lazy Lion was left outside by himself. The other animals listened to the

(8) _____ of thunder as Lazy Lion stood in the rain.

GET WISE TO TESTS

Directions: Read each sentence. Choose the word that best finishes the sentence. Mark the answer space for that word.

Tip Read carefully. Use the other words in the sentences to help you choose each missing word.

1. A _____ has many sharp teeth.
   ○ bird   ○ fish
   ○ snake   ○ crocodile

2. We sat on the _____ and had a picnic.
   ○ riverbank ○ plant
   ○ sky   ○ roof

3. _____ dig large holes to live in.
   ○ Cats   ○ Cattle
   ○ Aardvarks ○ Horses

4. Are you afraid of the _____ thunder?
   ○ talking   ○ rumbling
   ○ singing   ○ laughing

5. The duck _____ toward the water.
   ○ sat   ○ hopped
   ○ waddled   ○ danced

6. A _____ eats bees and honey.
   ○ duck   ○ person
   ○ sheep   ○ badger

7. You can drink through a straw because it is _____.
   ○ striped   ○ hollow
   ○ wet   ○ short

8. The _____ in the forest were afraid of people.
   ○ beasts   ○ cars
   ○ trees   ○ streams

Writing

In the story, Lazy Lion told each of the animals to build him a house. Do you think it was right for Lazy Lion to tell the other animals what to do? Why do you think this way?

On the lines below, write a letter to Lazy Lion telling him whether you think he should tell the other animals what to do and why. Use some vocabulary words in your writing.

_____
(date)

Dear Lazy Lion,

_____

_____

_____

_____

_____

_____

_____

_____

Your friend,

_____

Turn to "My Word List" on page 132. Write some words from the story or other words that you would like to know more about. Use a dictionary to find the meanings.

★ Read the story below. Think about the meanings of the words in **dark print**. ★

A Special Forest

You are in a forest. It is so dark you can barely see the tree trunks around you. Few plants grow on the ground, so it is easy to walk around. You can hear monkeys high above you. You're in a **rain forest**!

A rain forest can be found somewhere that is wet all year. The trees in the rain forest are always green. Some have beautiful flowers. **Fruit** grows on other trees. The fruit is food for the many animals in the rain forest. Some animals in the rain forest live their whole lives in the tops of the trees.

The trees in the rain forest are different **sizes**. Some are very tall, while others are shorter. Because of this, rain forests have several **levels**. The taller trees **form** the forest roof. The tops of shorter trees make a lower level. All the levels of tree **branches** keep light from getting to the forest floor.

Today the rain forests are in **danger**. People cut down the trees. **Pollution** kills the trees. If we don't work hard to save the rain forests, they might be lost forever.

Awareness

★ Go back to the story. Underline the words or sentences that give you a clue to the meaning of each word in **dark print**. ★

CONTEXT CLUES

Read each sentence. Look for clues to help you finish each sentence with a word from the box. Write the word on the line.

pollution	danger	fruit	levels
rain forest	branches	form	sizes

1. A _____ can be found somewhere that is warm and wet all year.

2. Animals of many _____ live in the rain forest.

3. The animals live on the different _____ of the rain forest.

4. Some walk and sleep on the _____ of the trees.

5. They eat _____ from the trees.

6. The tops of the trees _____ a kind of umbrella.

7. Things people do, such as driving cars, can cause _____.

8. Rain forests are in _____ because people keep cutting down the trees.

DICTIONARY SKILLS

Guide words are the two words at the top of each dictionary page. They show the first and last words on a page. All the words in between are in ABC order. Decide which word from the box would go on each page. Add a word that you know to each page.

branches	levels	fruit
pollution	danger	

apple/can

_____

_____

car/early

_____

_____

egg/good

_____

_____

keep/move

_____

_____

open/ran

_____

_____

Directions: Darken the answer space beside the word that best finishes the sentence.

Tip If you are not sure which word finishes the sentence, do the best you can. Try to choose the answer that makes the most sense.

1. A food that tastes sweet and grows on trees is . . .
   ○ paste   ○ fruit   ○ clothes   ○ candy

2. A very thick forest that grows where it is warm and wet is a . . .
   ○ dry forest   ○ cold forest   ○ rain forest   ○ snow forest

3. To tell how big things are, use . . .
   ○ sizes   ○ schools   ○ dresses   ○ toys

4. Something high and something low are on different . . .
   ○ roads   ○ rivers   ○ levels   ○ cars

5. To make is to . . .
   ○ break   ○ wash   ○ lift   ○ form

6. The parts of a tree that grow out from its trunk are . . .
   ○ branches   ○ leaves   ○ apples   ○ oranges

7. Something that can hurt you is a . . .
   ○ hope   ○ help   ○ danger   ○ thought

8. Something people do to hurt the earth is called . . .
   ○ plants   ○ pollution   ○ water   ○ air

Writing

Turn to "My Word List" on page 132. Write some words from the story or other words that you would like to know more about. Use a dictionary to find the meanings.

Pretend you just visited a rain forest. What plants and animals did you see? What sounds did you hear?

A diary is a book you can write your thoughts and feelings in. No one can read your diary unless you let them. On the lines below, write about your trip to the rain forest. Use some vocabulary words in your writing.

_____
(date)

Dear Diary,

_____

_____

_____

_____

_____

_____

_____

_____

_____

_____

_____

★ Read the story below. Think about the meanings of the words in **dark print**. ★

Time for Clocks

How can you tell the time? That's easy! You look at a clock. But long ago, there were no clocks. People **measured** time by looking at the sun. They knew how much time had gone by from how far the sun had moved in the sky.

The first clock was built in Italy. It was in the top of a tall **tower**. It didn't have hands. Instead, it rang a bell every **hour** of the day. Next, a man in Germany made a small clock using a spring made of **wire**. It had a hand that pointed to the hour. Then people in England began making tall clocks called **grandfather clocks**.

At about the same time, other people made clocks that could be carried in a pocket. These were the first watches. People had to **wind** the watches. They had to turn a button on the side so the watches wouldn't stop.

Today, most watches and clocks have two hands. One hand shows the hour. The other hand shows the parts of the hour, or **minutes**. Other clocks show the time in **numerals**, or written numbers. People from around the world made the clocks we use today.

★ Go back to the story. Underline the words or sentences that give you a clue to the meaning of each word in **dark print**. ★

USING CONTEXT

Meanings for the vocabulary words are given below. Go back to the story, and read each sentence that has a vocabulary word. If you still cannot tell the meaning, look for clues in the sentences that come before and after the one with the vocabulary word. Write each word in front of its meaning.

measured	numerals	hour	wire
grandfather clocks	minutes	wind	tower

1. _____ : a tall building

2. _____ : parts of an hour

3. _____ : written numbers

4. _____ : a thin piece of metal that looks like thread

5. _____ : tall wooden clocks that stand on the floor

6. _____ : found the size or amount of something

7. _____ : part of a day

8. _____ : to make a clock or watch go by turning a part of it

SYNONYMS

Synonyms are words that have the same or almost the same meaning. Read each pair of sentences. Circle the synonym in the second sentence for the underlined word in the first sentence.

1. José wrote a story about a clock <u>tower</u>.
   He wrote about a tall building with a clock.
2. The clock <u>measured</u> time.
   It told how much time had gone by.
3. This clock had a hand that pointed to the <u>hour</u>.
   The hand pointed to the part of the day.
4. This clock also had a hand that pointed to the <u>minutes</u>.
   This hand pointed to the parts of the hour.
5. People needed to <u>wind</u> this clock.
   Someone had to turn a part of the clock.
6. The clock was not like the <u>grandfather</u> <u>clocks</u> José had seen before.
   The tall wooden clocks were not as big as the clock in the tower.
7. These clocks made José think of his old watch, which had a spring made of <u>wire</u> inside.
   A thin piece of metal made his watch run.
8. But his new watch is different because it has <u>numerals</u>.
   It has written numbers instead of hands.

WORD CODES

A **code** is a kind of secret writing. Each number stands for a different letter.

A number is written below each answer space. Use the box at the bottom of the page to find out what letter each number stands for. Write your answer on the spaces above the numbers.

___ ___ ___ ___ ___ ___
3 12 15 3 11 19

___ ___ ___ ___ ___ ___
13 1 11 5 9 20

___ ___ ___ ___ ___ ___
5 1 19 25 20 15

___ ___ ___ ___ ___ ___ ___ ___
20 5 12 12 23 8 1 20

___ ___ ___ ___ ___ ___ ___ ___!
20 9 13 5 9 20 9 19

A=1	B=2	C=3	D=4	E=5	F=6	G=7
H=8	I=9	J=10	K=11	L=12	M=13	N=14
O=15	P=16	Q=17	R=18	S=19	T=20	U=21
V=22	W=23	X=24	Y=25	Z=26		

GET WISE TO TESTS

Directions: Look for the word or words that have the same or almost the same meaning as the underlined word. Mark the answer space for your choice.

Tip

Always read all the answer choices. Many choices may make sense. But only one answer choice has the same or almost the same meaning as the underlined word.

1. tall <u>tower</u>
   ○ building
   ○ car
   ○ flower
   ○ tree

2. the <u>hour</u> of noon
   ○ place
   ○ sound
   ○ time
   ○ thought

3. made of <u>wire</u>
   ○ water
   ○ grass
   ○ wood
   ○ metal

4. <u>wind</u> the toy
   ○ push
   ○ turn
   ○ break
   ○ paint

5. <u>parts</u> of an hour
   ○ cookies
   ○ plants
   ○ minutes
   ○ cars

6. <u>grandfather</u> clocks
   ○ tall clocks
   ○ small clocks
   ○ funny clocks
   ○ little clocks

7. read the <u>numerals</u>
   ○ letters
   ○ pictures
   ○ numbers
   ○ signs

8. <u>measured</u> the flour
   ○ found the amount
   ○ found the place
   ○ found the person
   ○ found the water

Writing

Many people in different countries helped to make clocks. Have you ever worked with others to make something? What did you make? Did working together make the job easier?

Use the lines below to write about what you made. Use some vocabulary words in your writing.

_____

_____

_____

_____

_____

_____

_____

_____

_____

_____

_____

Turn to "My Word List" on page 132. Write some words from the story or other words that you would like to know more about. Use a dictionary to find the meanings.

★ To review the words in Lessons 17–20, turn to page 129. ★

Read each clue. Then write the word from the box that fits the clue. Use the dictionary if you need help.

remember	crops	evil	costumes
brave	desert	pounced	flute

1. If you are not afraid, you can be called this.

   _____

2. People grow these. _____

3. This kind of place has very little water.

   _____

4. If you do not forget, you do this.

   _____

5. People wear these. _____

6. This is something people use to play music.

   _____

7. We use this word to describe something that

   is very bad. _____

8. If a tiger jumped on something, it

   did this. _____

Read the questions. Answer yes or no. Use the dictionary if you need help.

1. Do crowded people need to stand closer to each other? _____

2. Is medicine something you need when you are well? _____

3. Does a person need to know Spanish to understand it? _____

4. If the weather goes from sunny to rainy, does it change? _____

5. Would you find a satellite under your bed? _____

6. If you make laws, do you make rules? _____

7. Does a calm person run around and scream? _____

8. Is a flight something you can do in an airplane? _____

9. If your TV is working fine, do you need to repair it? _____

10. If you join a club, do you become part of it? _____

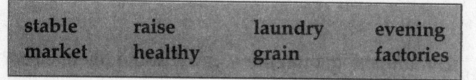

REVIEW

Read each clue. Then write the word from the box that fits the clue. Use the dictionary if you need help.

stable	raise	laundry	evening
market	healthy	grain	factories

1. When you eat oats, you are eating this.

   _____

2. It is dark outside at this time of day.

   _____

3. This is a place where people wash clothes.

   _____

4. Things are made in these places.

   _____

5. People can buy food at this kind of place.

   _____

6. A person who is not sick is this.

   _____

7. People keep horses in this kind of building.

   _____

8. We do this to crops and animals when we help them grow. _____

127

REVIEW

Read the questions. Answer yes or no. Use the dictionary if you need help.

1. Would a neighborhood fit inside your house?

   _____

2. Can people imagine they are somewhere else?

   _____

3. Do you have hundreds of toes on one foot?

   _____

4. Can people be cozy at home in bed? _____

5. Is it a good idea to talk to strangers? _____

6. Were you quiet if you howled? _____

7. To find a beaver's home, should you look for its lodge? _____

8. Are worker ants just like their queen?

   _____

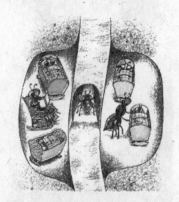

9. If you dragged a log, did you pull it? _____

10. If you need to raise your hand, should you lift it? _____

REVIEW

Read each clue. Then write the word from the box that fits the clue. Use the dictionary if you need help.

huge	danger	wind	beast
fruit	hollow	coast	measure

1. This is something sweet to eat.

   _____

2. You do this to make a watch go.

   _____

3. We use this word to describe very big things.

   _____

4. You do this to find the size of something.

   _____

5. This can be a mouse or an elephant.

   _____

6. This is where the land meets the sea.

   _____

7. When something is empty, it is this.

   _____

8. You should stay away from this.

   _____

REVIEW AND WRITE

You have read about many special people and places in this book. Remember Nellie Bly and Roberto Clemente, the ant colony, and the rain forest? Which special person or place did you like best? Why? Write about your choice. Use some vocabulary words you have learned.

_____

_____

_____

_____

_____

_____

_____

_____

_____

_____

_____

_____

_____

_____

This is your word list. Here you can write words from the stories. You can also write other words that you would like to know more about. Use a dictionary to find the meaning of each word. Then write the meaning next to the word.

UNIT 1
CELEBRATIONS

_____

_____

_____

_____

_____

_____

UNIT 2
HEROES

_____

_____

_____

_____

_____

_____

MY WORD LIST

UNIT 3
ON THE FARM

_____

_____

_____

_____

_____

UNIT 4
HOME SWEET HOME

_____

_____

_____

_____

_____

_____

UNIT 5
AROUND THE WORLD

_____

_____

_____

_____

_____

_____

DICTIONARY

A

aardvark, aardvarks An animal that digs a large hole to live in and eats ants. The **aardvark** is also called an anteater. page 108

adult, adults A person who is grown up. The **adult** watched the children swim. page 23

amazing Very surprising or wonderful. The rainbow was **amazing.** page 90

apart Not together. My best friend moved away, and now we live far **apart.** page 37

apartment, apartments A building with groups of rooms to live in. My friend Ben lives in an **apartment.** page 78

article A story written for a newspaper. I read an **article** in today's newspaper. page 30

astronaut A person who flies into space. I would like to be an **astronaut.** page 47

B

badger An animal that eats bees and honey. We saw a **badger** in the woods. page 108

banquet A big dinner for many people. They held a **banquet** for her birthday. page 13

battle A big fight with many people. The **battle** was fought in Mexico. page 6

beast, beasts Any animal with four legs. Have you seen that **beast?** page 108

beaver, beavers An animal with soft fur, a flat tail, and large front teeth. We saw a **beaver** yesterday. page 90

bedroom A room to sleep in. My **bedroom** is pink. page 78

block, blocks To stop something from passing by. The police will **block** the road so the parade can pass. page 90

branch, branches The part of a tree growing out from its trunk. We hung a swing from the **branch** of the tree. page 114

brave Not afraid. The **brave** man saved the little girl. page 6

C

calm Quiet and still. The girl read in a **calm** voice. page 37

carpenter, carpenters A person who builds and repairs wooden buildings. The **carpenter** built our new barn. page 90

change, changed, changing To become different. The weather will **change** tonight. page 36

chore, chores Work that must be done each day. Feeding the cat is my **chore**. page 54

clothing Clothes. Some people put their **clothing** in closets. page 66

coast The edge of land along the sea. I found some shells at the **coast**. page 102

colony A group of ants living together. I have an ant **colony** in my room. page 95

continent One of the seven large pieces of land on the earth. Have you ever visited the **continent** of Africa? page 102

coop A small cage or pen for chickens or other birds. We kept our hens in a **coop**. page 61

costume, costumes Special clothes worn for celebrations. Each person wore a **costume** for the dance. page 23

cozy Warm and dry. Maria was **cozy** under the blankets as she listened to the story. page 90

crash, crashed, crashing To fall down or to run into something. Watch where you are going, or you will **crash**. page 42

crocodile A large animal with many sharp teeth that lives near a river. We saw a **crocodile** at the zoo. page 109

crop, crops Plants that are grown for food. The corn **crop** will feed the animals. page 23

crowded Too close to each other. Two classes were **crowded** together in one room. page 30

D_____

dam A wall built to hold back water. The **dam** stopped the small stream. page 90

danger A chance of being hurt. You could be in **danger** if you speak to a stranger. page 114

decoration, decorations Something used to make a place look special. Balloons are a kind of **decoration.** page 12

describe, described, describing To tell about or write about. Please **describe** the dog. page 37

desert Land with little water. Few plants grow in the **desert.** page 18

diet The foods a person eats every day. I was on a special **diet** while I was sick. page 71

diner A small place to eat. We ate breakfast at a **diner.** page 84

dive, dives To jump into the water with the head first. Ming will **dive** into the water. page 18

drag, dragged, dragging To pull along. We can **drag** the box across the room. page 84

dream A wish. My **dream** is to become a teacher. page 37

dune, dunes A hill of sand. I saw a sand **dune.** page 102

E_____

earthquake A moving and shaking of the earth. The **earthquake** shook our house. page 42

elbow The place where the arm bends. Scan hurt his **elbow** when he fell. page 42

enemy, enemies A person or group who tries to hurt someone else. I don't think I have an **enemy.** page 90

energy The power to work. I can work all day since I have so much **energy.** page 71

envelope, envelopes A wrapper made of paper, used for mailing. I will mail my letter in a blue **envelope.** page 13

evening The time after the sun sets and before bedtime. I read every **evening.** page 60

evil Very bad. There is an **evil** witch in the story. page 12

excited Very happy. Heather was **excited** when her team won the game. page 36

exercise The moving of the body in work or play. She gets a lot of **exercise** when she plays tag. page 71

experiment, experiments A test that helps people find out about things. They did an **experiment** on plants and sunlight. page 47

F

factory, factories A place where things are made. We went to a **factory** that makes shoes. page 66

fair Right. The teacher is **fair** to students. page 30

farmer A person who works on a farm. My friend is a **farmer.** page 54

firecracker, firecrackers A paper tube that makes a loud noise when you light it. My uncle lit a **firecracker.** page 13

flight The act of flying. The **flight** into space is very long. page 47

flock A group of sheep or birds. **A flock** of geese flew over our house. page 54

flute A long, round piece of wood or metal that makes music. Do you know how to play the **flute?** page 18

fond Loving; liking. I am **fond** of my best friend. page 60

form To make. I will **form** a bowl from the clay. page 114

fruit A food that tastes sweet and grows on trees or bushes. An orange is a **fruit.** page 114

furniture The things in a house that can be moved. I have new **furniture** in my room. page 66

G

garden, gardens A piece of ground used for growing food or flowers. We grow peas and carrots in our **garden.** page 66

gobble, gobbled, gobbling To eat fast. We had to **gobble** our food so we could catch the school bus. page 84

grain The seed of wheat, oats, corn, and other cereal grasses. The farmer feeds **grain** to his cattle. page 71

grandfather clock, grandfather clocks A tall wooden clock that stands on the floor. We have a **grandfather clock.** page 119

graze, grazed, grazing To eat grass. My horse likes to **graze** in the field. page 54

grocery A store that sells food. We went to the **grocery** store. page 78

H

harvest The picking of crops. The wheat **harvest** always comes in the fall. page 71

healthy Not sick. Julio is a very **healthy** person. page 71

herd A group of large animals. I saw a **herd** of cattle. page 54

hollow Having nothing inside. The bees built a nest inside the **hollow** tree. page 108

hospital, hospitals A place where sick people are cared for. My aunt stayed in the **hospital** when she was sick. page 42

hour Part of a day. It took Heather one **hour** to do her homework. page 119

howl, howled, howling To make a long, loud cry. My dog can **howl** very loudly. page 85

huge Very large. Many dinosaurs were **huge.** page 102

hundred, hundreds 100. I can count to one **hundred** very easily. page 95

hut A small house. I built a **hut** from sticks and grass. page 23

I

imagine   To pretend or make a picture of something in the mind. **Imagine** yourself as a rabbit. page 84

J

join   To come into or come together with. Are you going to **join** the club? page 36

K

kangaroo, kangaroos   An animal in Australia that has strong back legs used for jumping. Is a **kangaroo** larger than a horse? page 102

kibbutz   A kind of farm in Israel. Many people live and work on a **kibbutz.** page 66

L

laundry   A room or building where clothes are washed. We took our dirty clothes to the **laundry.** page 66

law, laws   A rule made by a country or state for all the people who live there. There is a **law** in our city against stealing. page 30

level, levels   Tallness or shortness. At what **level** is the basketball net? page 114

lift   To pick up. My sister and I will **lift** the box. page 95

lodge   A home of sticks and mud built in a pond by beavers. The beavers were safe in their **lodge.** page 90

M

market   A place where farmers sell animals and other things. The farmer took some eggs to the **market.** page 54

mask, masks   A face made of wood or other things to be worn on special days. I wore a **mask** to the party. page 23

measure, measured, measuring   To find the size or amount of something. I will **measure** how tall you are. page 119

medicine Something a doctor gives you to help make you well. The doctor gave me **medicine** for my cold. page 42

member, members A person, animal, or thing belonging to a group. My sister is a **member** of that club. page 66

minute, minutes Part of an hour. One **minute** is a very short amount of time. page 119

munch To chew loudly. I could hear Sally **munch** the popcorn. page 84

N

neighbor, neighbors A person who lives in the next house or nearby. My **neighbor** has a large yard. page 78

neighborhood A place where people live near one another. My best friend lives in my **neighborhood.** page 78

newspaper Sheets of paper that tell about what just happened. I read the **newspaper.** page 30

numeral, numerals A written number. The teacher wrote the **numeral** 5. page 119

O

ocean, oceans A large body of salt water; the sea. I would like to see the **ocean.** page 102

P

pain A feeling of hurt. I have a **pain** in my knee. page 42

parent, parents A mother or father. Please ask a **parent** if you can go. page 6

pasture Grassy land that animals use for food. There are sheep in the **pasture.** page 54

perch Anything on which a bird can come to rest. The bird used the tree as a **perch.** page 61

pigpen A place where pigs are kept. My uncle has ten pigs in his **pigpen.** page 60

planet, planets A body in space that moves around the sun. The earth is a **planet.** page 47

playground   A place for outdoor play. We played on the swings at the **playground.** page 78

pollution   Something that people do to hurt the earth. **Pollution** is killing the fish in that river. page 114

pounce, pounced, pouncing   To jump on something suddenly and take hold. The kitten will **pounce** on anything. page 13

prance, pranced, prancing   To walk and dance. I **prance** when I am happy. page 13

protect   To keep from being hurt. **Protect** your head when you ride a bicycle. page 6

proud   Feeling good about who you are or something you have done. Juan was **proud** of his drawing. page 6

Q

queen   An ant that lays eggs. The worker ants care for the **queen.** page 95

R

rain forest   A very thick forest in a place where it is wet all year. I want to visit a **rain forest.** page 114

raise   To help something grow. My uncle likes to **raise** many kinds of flowers. page 54

remember   To think of something from the past; to keep in mind. Dora can **remember** the stories her grandfather told her. page 6

repair   To fix. My uncle knows how to **repair** a car. page 30

reporter   A person who writes for a newspaper. The **reporter** wrote a story about our school for the newspaper. page 30

rest   A state of sleeping. You need **rest.** page 71

restaurant   A place to buy and eat a meal. My parents took me to a **restaurant.** page 78

river, rivers   A large stream of water. We went fishing in the **river.** page 102

riverbank   The ground beside a river. We sat on the **riverbank** and ate sandwiches. page 109

roast, roasted, roasting   To cook in an oven. We decided to **roast** the chicken. page 85

ruler   Someone who leads a group of people. The king was the **ruler** of the country. page 6

rumbling   A deep, heavy sound. We heard the **rumbling** of thunder. page 109

S

safe   Free from danger. Our house is **safe.** page 30

satellite, satellites   A machine in space that sends pictures back to Earth. We saw pictures taken by a **satellite.** page 47

search   To look for something. I will **search** for my dog. page 18

shuttle   A spaceship with wings that can be used many times. The **shuttle** has gone into space many times. page 47

single   Only one. I saw a **single** flower under the tree. page 95

size, sizes   How big something is. What **size** shoe do you wear? page 114

soldier, soldiers   A person who fights in a group. The **soldier** was glad the war ended. page 6

spirit, spirits   A ghost. Some people believe that a **spirit** lives in that house. page 12

spring   Water that comes from the ground. Water from that **spring** runs into the river. page 18

stable   A building where horses or cattle are kept. They have horses in their **stable.** page 61

stampede, stampeded, stampeding   To run together when scared. The horses will **stampede** if they hear a loud noise. page 61

stranger, strangers   A person not known. We did not go near the **stranger.** page 78

study, studied, studying To try to learn about something. We will **study** subtraction. page 47

summer The warmest part of a year. I like **summer.** page 102

sunflower, sunflowers A large yellow flower that grows on a tall plant. There is a **sunflower** beside the house. page 18

symbol, symbols A picture or other thing that stands for something else. A horseshoe is a **symbol** of luck. page 18

T

tend To care for. I **tend** my garden every day. page 66

thousand, thousands 1,000. There were one **thousand** people there. page 95

tower A tall building. We could see the whole town from the top of the **tower.** page 119

tractor A machine used on a farm. The farmer drove the **tractor** across the field. page 71

trail A path in a wild area. A deer was on the **trail.** page 18

training Teaching. My dog needs some **training.** page 47

truth What is true. My sister always tells the **truth.** page 42

U

understand To know something. I **understand** math. page 42

upset Unhappy. He was **upset** when he fell. page 37

V

value, values What a person believes to be right and wrong. Each person has **values.** page 23

village A small town. Hoan visited a **village.** page 23

W

waddle, waddled, waddling
To walk with short steps. I
saw the ducks **waddle.**
page 109

weight How heavy
something is. The **weight** of
that package is three pounds.
page 95

western A story, movie, or
show about life in the western
part of the United States. We
watched a **western.** page 60

wheeze, wheezed, wheezing
To have a hard time
breathing. The dust made us
wheeze. page 84

wind To make a clock or
watch go by turning some
part of it. I will **wind** my
watch. page 119

wire A thin piece of metal
that looks like thread. The
fence was made of **wire.**
page 119

woodcarver A person who
makes things from wood. The
woodcarver made toys.
page 23

Y

year, years 12 months. I am
one **year** older today. page 95